THE JOY OF OWNING A SHIH TZU

Ch. Afshi's Gunther, owned by Joseph F. Joly, III and J. A. Torriello and bred by Marc Bowman and R. Charles, was campaigned for less than three years and achieved a record as the #2 top winning Shih Tzu dog of all time. He was campaigned by Dee Shepherd to a veritable galaxy of brilliant triumphs.

The JOY of Owning a
SHIH TZU

by ANN SERANNE
with LISE M. MILLER

Drawings by GLADYS RAY
Grooming photographs by ALAN MILLER

First Edition

HOWELL
BOOK HOUSE
New York

Macmillan General Reference
A Simon & Schuster Macmillan Company
1633 Broadway
New York, NY 10019-6785

Library of Congress Cataloging in Publication Data

Seranne, Anne, 1914–
  The joy of owning a shih tzu.

  1. Shih tzu.   I. Miller, Lise M.
II. Title.
SF429.S64S47   1982   636.7′6   82-11786
ISBN 0-87605-334-7

10   9   8

Printed in the United States of America

To
THE NEW BREEDERS
in whose hands
the future of the Shih Tzu lies

"Learn to Differentiate Between Better and Best,
not Between Good and Bad."

Stunning puppy, Luvncare Eric the Red, was sired by Can. Ch. Imua's Director of Luvncare, a great-grandson of "Pif." Eric was bred by Rosemarie Hoo of Brantford, Ontario,
Canada.

Contents

Ann Seranne

Lise M. Miller enjoying a private moment with a group of her Lisel Shih Tzu.

About the Authors

ANN SERANNE is acknowledged and celebrated in the purebred dog fancy for the quality of her animals, the depth of her knowledge and her precious ability to convey what she knows to others.

Of equal celebrity in the world of fine food and its preparation, Ann Seranne has helped make the American public more aware of haute cuisine and widening the American culinary repertoire. Her literary credits in the food sphere include *The New York Post*, where she was Food Editor, *Reader's Digest*, the National Broadcasting Company and Waring Products where she was a food consultant. She is the author and editor of numerous cook books and a contributor to *Family Circle* and other service magazines.

Her illustrious career also includes the post of Executive Editor for *Gourmet Magazine* and a partnership in the food publicity firm of Seranne and Gaden.

Ann Seranne has loved nature and animals all her life, so her progression to active membership in the dog sport was an easy extension of her feeling toward all living things. Pekingese were the first dogs in Ann's life, the first being a gift from her father when Ann was only seven. From that time until she came to live in New York City after World War II, Ann Seranne always had dogs as her constant companions.

In due course, her love of fine dogs led her into a partnership with Barbara Wolferman and the Mayfair-Barban Yorkshire Terriers were officially launched. Now situated on an 11-acre ranch in the mountains of northern New Jersey, Ann Seranne could finally give her creative talent and flair for dogs free rein.

Ann eventually became the co-breeder and/or owner of more than 60 Yorkshire Terrier champions including six multiple BIS winners and a half dozen Standard Poodle title holders including two multiple BIS dogs.

This great lady of the fancy came under the spell of the *lion dog* in 1968 when Mayfair's Kennel Manager, Peter D'Auria, acquired a gold and white yearling that grew up to be Ch-Si-Kiang's Mayfair Geisha. A year after "Gay" finished her championship, Barbara presented Ann with the blue-black charmer, Si-Kiang's Barban Chee Chee. Although she never finished, Chee Chee had two litters and became the dam and grand-dam of champions. Chee Chee continues at Mayfair as the official "greeter" and "house mother."

Enchantment led to increasing interest that had as its ultimate result this book. *The Joy of Owning a Shih Tzu* is the most recent in a list of writing credits for Ann Seranne that includes columns in *Pure-Bred Dogs—American Kennel Gazette* and *Kennel Review* as well as the books *All About Small Dogs in the Big City* and the superlative *The Joy of Breeding Your Own Show Dog.*

Ann Seranne, an AKC approved judge of a number of Toy and Non-Sporting breeds, is especially popular in the Shih Tzu fancy as an authority who knows this breed especially well.

LISE M. MILLER is typical of the energetic enthusiastic people that make up the modern Shih Tzu fancy in the United States.

A graduate of the University of Connecticut and Katherine Gibbs Secretarial School, Mrs. Miller is with the Accounting Department of Thyssen Environmental Systems Corporation.

On her own time Lise Miller is deeply involved in the betterment of the Shih Tzu as well as his advancement and protection. It takes a special kind of person to hold the purse strings for a national club and Lise Miller is just such a one, serving as Treasurer for the American Shih Tzu Club at this writing. She has also occupied the same position for the Shih Tzu Club of Northern New Jersey.

Very much committed to the role of the breeder in the dog game, Lise Miller sets a graphic example through her own dogs. Fully six of the present household population of the Lisel Shih Tzu are homebred champions—a commendable achievement.

As this book goes to press Shih Tzu have competed as a recognized breed in the United States for about 13 years and Lise Miller has conducted an active breeding program for more than ten of those 13 years. One of Lise's proudest achievements is her handling the cover dog of this book, Ch. Lisel's Rock N' Rye, to his championship entirely from the Bred-by-Exhibitor class. This was but the second time in the history of the breed that a dog reached championship status via the difficult, but rewarding, "Bred-by" road.

Lise Miller also owns two Shih Tzu bitches that have reached #1 status in the breed in both America and Continental Europe and has judged at all-breed matches and Specialty events.

Her special feeling for the breed can be observed in many places throughout this book, and especially in the grooming chapter where she and the Lisel Shih Tzu served as photographer's models.

The Shih Tzu is fortunate to have Lise Miller as a supporter and can only benefit further from the association in the years ahead.

10

Foreword

BECAUSE THE DOG FANCY NEEDED a practical book on breeding, whelping and caring for puppies, we asked Ann Seranne to provide a text that would fill this very important need. The result of her labors, *The Joy of Breeding Your Own Show Dog*, has admirably fulfilled all the hopes the author and ourselves had for it.

Happily the *joy* didn't stop with the publication of Ann's nonpareil breeding opus. Now comes *The Joy of Owning a Shih Tzu*, a many-faceted superlative study of this endearing Toy dog in the modern world. Written with the help of Lise Miller, this book provides important information for veteran and newcomer and adds significantly to the available literature on the breed.

For the person enamoured of "the lion dog of Peking," and considering adding a Shih Tzu to his or her life, there is important, practical guidance on how to go about finding the right puppy, what to expect from the seller and what is expected of the buyer. The new owner, likewise will find a wealth of information essential to successfully keeping and rearing of these elegant little dogs. Many little things can make a tremendous difference in dog/owner relationships when they are correctly applied. Here you will learn how to apply them.

For the Shih Tzu owner who would like to have a try at the wonderful world of the show ring, there are chapters on what is involved. A special chapter on the Shih Tzu in obedience demonstrates

11

that the breed has a natural aptitude for the work and can hold his own against all comers.

And for all lovers of the breed, many special joys await. Here you will encounter the Shih Tzu's intriguing, often spectacular, history before and after AKC recognition. Here are the stories behind the breed leaders and their inspiring determination to bring their favorite to the heights of fame. The movers and shakers in Canada and the United States take the spotlight and give every reader a better chance to know more about the breed and its people than ever before.

A chapter on color inheritance in the Shih Tzu is an important plus and truly fascinating. Serious breeders will treasure it and casual owners will be intrigued and enthralled by it. Truly this is the key to the "Shih Tzu rainbow!"

The text throughout is enhanced by a dazzling gallery of beautiful pictures in crisp black and white and vivid color. These photographs depict many of the breed's finest examples from every corner of the world. This book is a feast for the eye as for the mind.

A further bonus for the student is the presentation of many important pedigrees. Here are the lines of descent from the early greats to contemporary top producers. It's a reference every serious Shih Tzu breeder will treasure and use often.

And running through the book like a continuous strand is the obvious love of and concern for the breed shown by Ann Seranne and Lise Miller. From first page to last, these ladies—one an active judge and the other an active breeder/exhibitor—present an approach to the Shih Tzu that is enjoyable, refreshing and learned.

We were impressed with the energy and dedication that resulted in *The Joy of Breeding Your Own Show Dog.* We are newly delighted to find the same energy, dedication and devotion to enhancing fanciers' knowledge in *The Joy of Owning a Shih Tzu.* Accordingly, we are as proud to bring this writing achievement to you as Ann Seranne and Lise Miller were to prepare it.

—THE PUBLISHERS

Shih Tzu "Talk"

In the dog fancy, as in most other specialized endeavors, there is a particular lexicon very familiar to regulars but confusing to outsiders and newcomers. You will come across many of these words as you read *The Joy of Owning a Shih Tzu*. You will also encounter abbreviations for words and terms commonly used by dog people. The following list is included to help you with some of the language of the dog game.

The name Shih Tzu is singular *and* plural and is pronounced Shi*d* Zoo.

Abbreviations used in this book
AKC   The American Kennel Club
CKC   The Canadian Kennel Club
ASTC   The American Shih Tzu Club
BIS   Best in Show
BB   Best of Breed
BOS   Best of Opposite Sex
BW   Best of Winners
WD   Winners Dog
WB   Winners Bitch
Am. Bred.   American Bred
BBE   Bred by Exhibitor
Toy Grp. (1,2,3,4)   Placing won in the Toy Group
BIM   Best in Match Show   Norw.   Norwegian
BISS   Best in Specialty Show   Fin.   Finnish
CC   Challenge Certificate   Germ.   Germany
Ch. Champion (American)   C.D.   Companion Dog
R.O.M.   Registry of Merit   C.D.X.   Companion Dog Excellent
Can.   Canadian   U.D.   Utility Dog
Mex.   Mexican
Ber.   Bermuda
Eng.   English
Swed.   Swedish
Int. Ch.   International Champion

Si Kiang Mayfair Chee Chee, co-owned by the author, illustrates the *dash of teddy bear*, as she snuggles in the arms of celebrated comedienne Mary Wicks, frequent visitor to Mayfair.

A basket of black-masked, gold and white puppies just twelve weeks old. They were bred by Barbara Ward, Revere, Mass., who called them The E'zee Bunch after their sire, Ch. Winemakers E'zee Luvin'. Not all will be show quality just because daddy was. Those that are not will be sold as pets to loving homes.

14

1

Is a Shih Tzu For You?

In 1971, two years after the American Kennel Club recognized the Shih Tzu as a distinct and different breed, James E. Mumford wrote in the *Shih Tzu News* that he had learned more about the origin of the breed from his dog Choo Choo than from breed historians.

Although undoubtedly of Tibetan and Chinese origin, he surmised, "no one knows how the eunuchs in their palace experiments added a dash of lion, several teaspoons of rabbit, a couple of ounces of old men (Chinese), a bit of beggar, a tablespoon of monkey, one part baby seal and a dash of teddy bear."

Certainly no one could give a more apt description than that of the diversified charms and personality of the Shih Tzu.

And yet . . . as fascinating and enchanting as the Shih Tzu may be . . . it just may not be the right breed for you.

If you are ready to buy a purebred dog, take plenty of time to decide which breed will best suit your personality and your life style. You're not buying a new coat that can be discarded when it no longer suits you. You are investing in a bundle of living energy, built as you are of tissue, bone and muscle and you owe it the love, attention and care it needs to develop its instinctive personality and charm.

So if you are not absolutely certain in your mind that a Shih Tzu is the RIGHT breed for you, don't even look at a litter of puppies. All

Don't go to see any of these "fluffy little people" with soulful eyes, unless you've decided the Shih Tzu is the breed for you. These irresistible gold and white parti-colored puppies, just ten weeks old were bred by Betty Neilsen, Warren, Pa. *Neilsen*

Typical of the Oriental expression and "chrysanthemum stage," that Shih Tzu puppies go through from three to four months, Topper of Shang T'ou, just 11 ½ weeks old, was bred by pioneer breeder Eleanor Eldredge. *Eldredge*

At four months this charmer has enough head fall to sport a bow. It is Barber's Mai Ling of Shang T'ou owned by Larry & Marci Barber and bred by Eleanor Eldredge. *Eldredge*

16

puppies are adorable from eight to twelve weeks, the time that most breeders place pet-quality puppies in good homes. But a Shih Tzu puppy is particularly beguiling, an irresistible ball of animated fluff, guaranteed to steal your heart in short order. Few can resist the appeal of those dark brown, sparkling eyes, peering meltingly from a shaggy head that looks like an enormous chrysanthemum.

The Shih Tzu, pronounced *Shid Zoo*, whether referring to one or to many, is a small, sturdy, heavily-coated Toy dog of ancient origin. The adult will weigh in at from nine to fifteen pounds. Over the centuries it was developed and bred strictly for loving. It is regal and dignified, but at the same time playful, lovable, huggable and self-assured. It bursts into a room with enthusiastic exuberance, demands that its presence be acknowledged, then stretches out on its favorite chair or couch, satisfied to be in the company of loved ones.

More than most breeds, the Shih Tzu thrives on family companionship and, without it, life to a Shih Tzu is just not worth living.

The Shih Tzu is seldom shy and is generally good-natured even under stressful conditions. Unlike many other breeds, Shih Tzu enjoy each other without scrapping. Should an occasional spat occur, it is over almost as soon as it starts with no grudges held. They retain their youthful spirit well into old age, but spend long periods in deep meditation, like small Buddhas. They do not mind being left alone all day (a great asset for single, working people), yet would prefer the companionship of another dog or even a cat to being left alone with their toys. Toys are great fun, but poor substitutes for a warm, living animal or human playmate.

Shih Tzu will sound a warning when a stranger appears or there is a knock on the door, but they are not yappers and, once they know a person is friend rather than foe, will turn on the charm and captivate the visitor in a short time.

Shih Tzu can be just as happy in a high-rise apartment in the center of a throbbing metropolis as in a suburban or urban community. They adjust readily to almost any home situation but are, essentially just that—house dogs and companions *par excellence*. They must not be turned loose in the yard or left alone with young children. They are extremely intelligent, obedient and easily taught to be good canine members of the community, providing you know how to teach them their manners. They love long walks and enjoy riding in the car in cool weather.

Those are the virtues of the Shih Tzu and they are many. On the negative side, you must remember they are a long-haired breed, and so require extensive coat care. If you do not enjoy grooming a dog or appreciate the beauty of a coat which, when mature, will be long and luxuriant, you'd be better to consider a short-haired breed. If you are

The coat on the head continues to grow and by five months is long enough to be caught up by an elastic band into a "waterfall" topknot. Fancee Endear Ring of Bon D'Art, or "Dearie," is beginning to grow out of the chrysanthemum stage into a lovely Oriental-looking young lady. She was bred by Bonnie Guggenheim and Dolly Wheeler and is owned by Ruth Woodward.

There are dedicated breeders in every state of the Union and in Canada today, and from them you can be sure of a quality puppy. These typical little beauties were bred by Virginia Coughlan, Gibar Shih Tzu, Anchorage, Alaska.

busy caring for small children and will not have time for the daily combing and brushing a Shih Tzu requires, settle for a larger breed, sufficiently agile to get out from under small feet, and save the joy of owning a Shih Tzu until your children are grown and you have more time to appreciate and care for one.

But back to the positive side, Shih Tzu are fastidious in their personal habits and their non-shedding coats have no doggy odor if given a weekly bath to keep coat and skin clean.

When you are absolutely, positively sure that the Shih Tzu will be your ideal companion dog, visit the homes or kennels of reputable breeders in your area. Write to the American Kennel Club, 51 Madison Avenue, New York, N.Y. 10010 for a list of such breeders or for the name of the Secretary of the American Shih Tzu Club, who will quickly respond. Just be sure to enclose a self-addressed, stamped envelope.

Don't begin to look for a bargain or a "cheap" Shih Tzu puppy— shelters and pounds are full of inexpensive dogs, many of which are devastatingly appealing and desperately need good homes. When buying a purebred, like most of the other good things in life, you get what you pay for. And you are sure to get better quality from one who is breeding for future show champions than from a puppy mill or pet shop, where the only concern is a fast turnover of living merchandise for the quickest buck possible.

There is a host of dedicated Shih Tzu breeders, working hard to keep the breed both physically and mentally sound as well as handsome, breeding always to a Standard of Perfection approved by the American Kennel Club. Working with fine dogs is an expensive hobby, and the price you pay for a puppy is only a drop in the overall financial bucket that a dedicated breeder must carry.

From such a source you can be sure of a well-bred, carefully raised and conditioned puppy, free of external and internal parasites. Such a puppy will have been immunized against dangerous canine diseases, and usually the asking price is more than fair. You will have a healthy, happy, carefree puppy, the result of many generations of high-quality ancestors. It will lavish love on you and ask only that you love and care for it in return.

Some breeders will require you to sign an agreement that permits them to withold registration papers until proof of spaying or neutering is received. You are buying a lovely puppy purely as a pet. Don't expect to get show or breeding quality at pet price. If you don't plan to show or breed, the well-bred pet will give you as much pleasure as any show prospect.

Ch. Samalee's Precious Golden Girl, bred by Ron and Marnie Oystrick, completed her championship by winning best of opposite sex at a national Specialty over a record-breaking entry. She is shown here just as she is growing out of the "chrysanthemum stage."

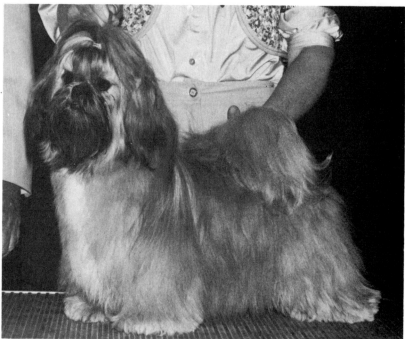

Shih Tzu compete in the Non-Sporting Group in Canada. Ch. Samalee's Cracklin' Rose is just 11 months old as she walks off with her championship and Best Puppy in Group. She is owned and was bred by Marnie Oystrick.

20

2

How It All Began—The Origin of the Shih Tzu From Tibet to America

UNDOUBTEDLY OF ANCIENT ORIGIN, the roots of our present day Shih Tzu are deeply veiled by the cobwebs of time. By putting together fragments of history, we can speculate that their first home was Tibet, and that they were the smallest of the Tibetan breeds, which include the Lhasa Apso, the Tibetan Terrier, the Chow Chow and the Tibetan Mastiff. Here they were bred by Buddhist monks in the temples and were prized by the Dalai Lamas as "holy dogs."

The Shih Tzu in the Orient

Small dogs in assorted shapes and colors had been bred in China for centuries, but it was not until Peking was captured by the Manchus in 1644 that small dogs, which could have been the prototype of early Shih Tzu, were bred by the eunuchs in the Imperial palaces. Prior to this time we find references to short-headed, short-legged "Pai" dogs as early as the 11th Century, and in the 13th Century golden-coated dogs were described and were treasured in the courts. However, cats were more in favor than dogs until 1850 when several of the Tibetan temple dogs were sent as tribute gifts to Manchu Emperors in the palaces in Peking. The Chinese called them Tibetan *Shih Tzu Kou* or "Lion Dogs." *Shih Tzu* means lion and *Kou* is the Chinese word for dog. According to English naturalist, Brian Vesey-Fitzgerald, the Chinese often clipped their Shih Tzu to look like little lions.

In 1908, some small shaggy dogs of the Shih Tzu type were presented to the Dowager Empress Tzu Hsi by the spiritual leader of the Tibetan people, the Dalai Lama.

It was well known that the Empress was a keen dog fancier and an avid breeder of Pekingese. Until the fall of the Manchu Dynasty in 1912, three varieties of small lion dogs were bred by the eunuchs in the Imperial Palaces in Northern China. These were the Pekingese, the short-haired Pug and the long-haired Shih Tzu. All were short-nosed breeds and, at the time, did not vary as much in shape as in quality and length of coat.

As long as breeding activities were supervised by the old Dowager Empress, they were strictly controlled and the breeds were kept as distinct as possible. Tzu Hsi considered the Shih Tzu Kou a valuable and most treasured gift from the Grand Priest, and she kept them well apart from her precious Pekingese in order to maintain the individual breed characteristics. She was particularly interested in color breeding, preferring the honey or "Imperial Gold," and in symmetry of markings. A white splash on the forehead of a Shih Tzu Kou was considered one of the superior markings of Buddha.

After the death of the Dowager Empress in 1908, the palace eunuchs continued breeding to a lesser degree and it is more than likely that many experimental cross breedings were conducted, resulting in divergencies in type, structure and size. Unwanted genes were injected into the three different types which can continue to surface even today in close breedings. The eunuchs kept no records or pedigrees and their breeding practices were closely-kept secrets. Illustrated scrolls were used on which outstanding specimens were depicted, and the eunuchs considered it a great honor for their charges to be worthy of portrayal on an Imperial scroll.

But gradually the foundation stock of the Empress became dissipated and diffused. Dogs of inferior type were sold in the market place; others were smuggled out of the palace and sold to Chinese noblemen or to visiting foreigners, and a great deal of confusion existed as to which breed was really which.

In 1923 the China Kennel Club was formed in Shanghai and classed all these small dogs as Lhasa Terriers or Tibetan Poodles, but in 1934 the Peking Kennel Club was established and scheduled classes at their shows for Lhasa Lion Dogs. Shih Tzu were shown in these classes but were divided by size; those up to 12 pounds and those over 12 pounds. The following Standard was used to judge both classes.

Standard Features of the Shih Tzu (Peking Kennel Club, 1938)

Lion Head: Long ears—heart-shaped (the longer the hair the better on the ears).

Long Apron and Pantaloons: (Long hair difficult to get on hind legs and all the more appreciated).

Weight: 10 to 15 pounds.

Height: 9 to 12 inches.

Eyes: Large and clear (the hair should fall over them and cover them completely if possible).

Toes: Well-feathered; paws broad and flat.

Front Legs: May be slightly bowed (controversy about this).

Hindquarters: Slightly higher than the back.

Hair: As glossy as possible. Apron and pantaloons wavy.

Skull: Broad and flat.

Nose: Deep stop; medium flat.

Tail: Well-plumed; carried gaily over the back.

Colors: All colors permissible, single and mixed, tawny or honey-colored highly favored.

The Shih Tzu in France

The Comte and Comtesse d'Anjou, who had raised Shih Tzu in Peking for many years prior to the invasion, devised the French Standard which received the approval of the Ambassador of France and Paraguay. The Ambassador had also spent many years in China, had owned a large number of Tibetan Lion Dogs and had judged them at Peking dog shows.

The French Standard of the Shih Tzu (Lion Dog of Tibet)

Characteristics: These are very heavily coated dogs, with a distinctly arrogant carriage, very active and lively, full of independence and courage. They are very affectionate and have a lot of personality. They are brave, but do not search for trouble. They take correction without batting an eyelid as if they do not understand why they are being punished. They have the habit of sleeping on their tummies, the paws stretched out before and behind, so that it is difficult to distinguish head from tail, the coat being thick and abundant.

Body: Length from withers to root of tail; considerably longer than height at withers, well ribbed-up, lower in front than behind. The opposite is a serious fault.

Coat: Woolly undercoat and a top-coat which is long, fine and silky, non-wavy and falls to the ground in the most beautiful specimens.

23

Neck: Short and strong.

Apron and Breeches: Well-furnished and long, making the most typical feature in the silhouette of those dogs.

Colour: (Same as the English with this addition). Honey-coloured and white are rare and much appreciated.

Weight: For preference between 11 and 14 pounds.

Scale of Points: General appearance, 20. Head, 15. Balance, 20. Coat, 30. Tail, 15.

By comparing the Standards of Peking and France with the Standard used originally in England for breeding, one can see the attempt to change the Shih Tzu to a better and more distinctive type.

The Shih Tzu Arrives in England

Initial interest in the Shih Tzu in England commenced in 1930. Several shaggy dogs were imported from China by General Sir Douglass and Lady Brownrigg. Although classed as "Apsos," it was quite obvious to the initiated, when they made their appearance in the show ring, that they were a similar but different breed. Although their shaggy coats resembled that of the Lhasa Apso, their noses were much shorter and so were their legs, while their skulls were considerably wider. Also, the Brownriggs' dogs were smaller and more compact with faces like "chrysanthemums."

In 1933 a few Shih Tzu were shown at the Cheltenham show, and the following year, the Kennel Club permitted the Apso and Lion Dog Club to change its name to Shih Tzu (Tibetan Lion Dog) Club. Soon after this, the club ruled that the dogs from China were not Apsos, but were Shih Tzu. By 1935 the Tibetan Lion Dog part of the name was omitted and the Shih Tzu Club of England was born under the Presidency of the Countess of Essex, with Lady Brownrigg serving as Secretary.

During the next four years the club thrived and grew strong until the outbreak of war in September 1939. World War II seriously curtailed all purebred dog activity in Britain for ten years and, although the Shih Tzu breed was granted a separate register on May 7, 1940, and became eligible for Challenge Certificates, none were awarded until 1949.

The first English champion was Lady Brownrigg's Ch. Ta Chi of Taishan. Other Shih Tzu owned by the Brownriggs were Hibou, Shu Ssa, Yangtse and Tzu Hsi. They acquired their first pair when the General was stationed in Peking, Hibou was a dog, and Shu Ssa was a bitch. Shu Ssa had her first litter by Hibou in China and her second litter, also by Hibou, when she was in quarantine upon their return to England. Yangtse was born in this second litter and Tzu Hsi was whelped sometime later.

Hibou and Shu Ssa, along with another Shih Tzu dog imported from China by Miss Madeleine Hutchins, Lung-Fu-Sssu, to Ireland became the foundation stock of present day Shih Tzu and the well-known Taishan strain, and may be found at the beginning of almost every extended pedigree. Later imports were bred back to the original strain to consolidate type.

Other imported dogs which were successfully bred from are: Tashi of Chouette, a bitch brought to England by the Earl of Essex in 1938, Choo-Choo, a dog, presented to Her Majesty the Queen Mother in 1933, and three bitches imported by Gen. Telfer Smollett: Ming, 1939, Ishuh Tzu, 1948, and Hsing-Erh, 1952.

From 1930 to the end of 1955, nearly 700 Shih Tzu were registered with the Kennel Club. The breed was exported to America, Canada, Australia and many countries in Europe where they were shown and bred.

Championship status was granted in 1940, when most of the Shih Tzu in England were conforming to the original type. By 1956 thirteen dogs held the championship title. These were:

Ch. Ta Chi of Taishan (b)
Ch. Pa-Ko of Taishan (b)
Ch. Yu Mo Chuang of Boydon (d)
Ch. Choo-Ling (d)
Ch. Sing-Tzu of Shebo (b)
Ch. Shebo Tsemo of Lhakang (d)
Ch. Mao-Mao of Lhakang (b)
Ch. Tensing of Lhakang (d)
Ch. Ling-Fu of Shuanghsi (b)
Ch. Hong of Hungjao (d)
Ch. Maya Wong of Lhakang (b)
Ch. Wang-Poo of Taishan (d)
Ch. Yi Ting Mo of Antarctica (d)

Audrey Dadds, in her charming book, *The Shih Tzu,* gives Lady Brownrigg credit for naming the Shih Tzu the ''chrysanthemum'' dog. Almost thirty years after she brought her first pair, she described Shu Ssa as follows:

"She was white with a black patch on her side, root of tail and head. This had a white topknot or applemark. Her hair was not as long as it became, but it stuck up all round her face, and with her large eyes she looked like a fluffy baby owl or perhaps a chrysanthemum!" A most appropriate and descriptive name for the Shih Tzu breed.

Another person who was captivated by the charm of the Shih Tzu was Mrs. Audrey Fowler. During the winter of 1936-37 she went to China and on route there she tried to obtain one. She made many expeditions to weird quarters of Hong Kong and Shanghai where she met many rickshaw boys saying with their usual cheerful smile, "We find you little doggie!" But they never did.

When she arrived in Peking, she met the Comtesse d'Anjou, and there in the courtyard of her house in Legation Street were her dream dogs—small honey-and-gold-colored shaggy dogs. The Comtesse had only one golden and white female puppy of the right age to undertake the strenuous journey back to England, but finally she was able to find a second dog, a little honey-colored bitch from another breeder. She brought these two Shih Tzu back to England with her in 1937 and was one of the last fanciers to have seen the breed in China. She treasures the registration cards from the Peking Kennel Club of her first two Shih Tzu—Nui San and Fu Tzu.

In England Mrs. Fowler was one of the few breeders to breed for a clear, deep gold, and she exported some of the first Shih Tzu to the United States. Both Maureen Murdock, one of the earliest breeders in America, and Mary Frothingham bought their original breeding and show stock from Mrs. Fowler.

We know of two other Shih Tzu that came out of China in 1949. A British couple, who were fleeing from China just before the advance of the Red Army, took with them a lovely, camel-colored dog with a luxuriant coat, called Wuffles, the other Mai-Ting, a black and white bitch. Mai Ting was bred to Wuffles and a single black and white puppy was whelped in October, 1950. A couple of years later, Wuffles was tragically killed by a truck.

The last recorded Shih Tzu to leave China was a bitch, Hsi-Li-Ya, imported to England by a Mr. Dobson in 1952. None of these dogs contributed much, if anything, that we know of to the Shih Tzu breed.

Photographs of many of these early dogs may be found in *This is the Shih Tzu*, by Reverend D. Allan Easton and Joan McDonald Brearley.

Post-War England and the Pekingese Cross

After the war, Lady Brownrigg helped the Shih Tzu Club to become active again. Many new breeders were attracted to the enchanting little dogs and many litters were registered with the Kennel Club.

Leading kennels during the 1950s, which left their mark on present day Shih Tzu were Taishan (Lady Brownrigg), Lhakang (Mrs. Widdrington), Antarctica (Mr. & Mrs. K. B. Rawlings) and Elfann (Freda Evans) and a good deal of exchange breeding took place between these kennels.

It was during this important decade of the Shih Tzu in England that the controversial Pekingese cross was made by Freda Evans who, in addition to breeding Shih Tzu, was a well-known, active breeder of Elfann Pekes.

26

A rare photograph of Mrs. Audrey Fowler with three generations of her Chasmu Shih Tzu. A black-masked gold puppy sits between its grandsire, Chasmu Solo, gold and white (right) and its black-masked father, Hortion Lee of Chasmu. Mrs. Fowler was in her 80s when this picture was taken at the 1964 Connecticut Yankee Shih Tzu match. Picture, courtesy of Mat (Mary) Frothingham.

**PEDIGREE OF CHASMU SOLO, dog, White/Gold/Brindle, bred by Mrs.
A. Fowler, owned in the United States by Mrs. N. Frothingham.**

Ch. Golden Peregrine of Elfann

Cherholmes Garcon of Chasmu

Cherholmes Debutante

Ho Kwang of Chasmu

Yuk Cham of Chasmu

Cheng Ting Ting of Chasmu

Yeshonala of Chasmu

CHASMU SOLO

Ch. Golden Peregrine of Elfann

Cherholmes Garcon of Chasmu

Cherholmes Debutante

Su So of Chasmu

Te Ching of Chasmu

Mara of Chasmu

Cheng Ting Ting of Chasmu

27

As a result, this acknowledged cross, and many others which were undoubtedly made in England surreptitiously and without record, introduced the bowed leg recessive into the genetic structure of the Shih Tzu. On the positive side is the fact that Shih Tzu twenty years after the cross was made were more uniform in size. Yet bowed front legs continue to appear and persist in many lines today.

The blame for this structural fault cannot be placed entirely on Freda Evans' shoulders, since the original Peking Standard, written in 1938 allowed "slightly bowed front legs," probably due to the unsupervised and secretive breedings of the eunuchs remaining in the Imperial palace after the death of the Empress Tzu Hsi. We know that we can breed away from recessive genes, whether these are faults or virtues, but, once introduced, they are carried along from generation to generation in the genotype *ad infinitum*, and can surface when least expected.

The Pekingese selected by the knowledgeable Miss Evans, Philadelphus Suti-T'son of Elfann, was an excellent specimen in every way, except one—he had straight front legs! He was bred to Elfann Fenling of Yram.

In England the third generation offspring or F_3 from the original cross was recognized by the Kennel Club and could be shown there. In the past, the American Kennel Club has required another three generations to pass before any dogs directly related to an approved cross could be registered.

It is interesting to note, however, that in 1981, the Board of Directors approved the registration of fifth generation offspring of an experimental Dalmatian-Pointer cross begun in 1973 by Dr. Robert Schaible, a geneticist and Dalmatian breeder, in an attempt to eventually eliminate a serious genetic defect that appeared to be present in all Dalmatians at that time.

Three bitches and two dogs were third generation offspring of the Pekingese-Shih Tzu cross. This generation was bred by a Miss O.I. Nichols of Devon, who owned the 2nd generation cross-bred dam, Yu-Honey of Elfann. Two of the three bitches, Michelcombe Dinkums and Michelcombe Fucia remained with their breeder, the third bitch, Elfann Shih-Wei-Tzu was transferred to Mrs. Murray Kerr in Scotland. The dogs were Ti-Ni-Tim of Michelcombe, transferred to Mrs. Widdrington in England, and Mu-Ho, registered by Mrs. Thelma Moran of the Midlands.

The progeny of these F_3 offspring were distributed throughout the country, so that before long it became almost impossible to find foundation breeding stock that was not directly or indirectly the result of the Pekingese cross.

28

The Pekingese/Shih Tzu Cross

Pu of Oulton

    Ch. Hong of Hungjao

        Sing Pu

Fu Chuan of Elfann

        Wu Chow of Shuanghsi

    Chuanne Tu of Elfann

        Elfann Fenling of Yram

3 bitches, 2 dogs (see above)

        Sanus Ching-A-Boo

    Ch. Loo-Ling

        Sing Pu

Yu Honey of Elfann

        Philadelphus Suti-T'sun of
          Elfann (Pekingese)

    Yu Sunny of Elfann

        Elfann Fenling of Yram

THIRD GENERATION F_3

$\frac{1}{16}$ **Pekingese**

    SECOND GENERATION F_2

    $\frac{1}{8}$ **Pekingese**

        FIRST GENERATION F_1

        $\frac{1}{4}$ **Pekingese**

The Shih Tzu Arrives in Norway

At about the same time as the Shih Tzu were becoming known in England, Mrs. Henrick Kauffman, wife of the Danish Minister to China, transferred three Shih Tzu to the Danish Legation in Oslo from Peking, and registered them with the Norwegian Kennel Club in 1934.

It is quite possible, if you trace back far enough in the pedigrees of present day American Shih Tzu, you'll run across the names of these early progenitors. They were Aidzo, a dog, out of Lun-Geni by Law-Hu that was born in Imperial Peking, Schauder, a bitch out of Aidzo-Huh by Hu-Luh that was born in Imperial Shanghai, and Leidza another bitch out of Chin-Tai by Wu Hi, that according to authorities, was bred and whelped right in the Imperial Palace in Peking. These three dogs were the foundation of the Shih Tzu breed in Scandinavian countries and Leidza is supposed to be the only direct link back to the Palace-bred Shih Tzu Kou.

The Shih Tzu Arrives in Sweden

Walter Ekman was the pioneer breeder in Sweden. Returning from a trip to China he brought home with him a male Shih Tzu.

In 1939 he imported a bitch named Amoy from Lady Brownrigg in England to breed to him. Amoy was sired by Tangtz of Taishan out of Tzu Hsi of Taishan. This was the beginning of the breed in Sweden.

Many years later, in 1955, Mrs. Erma Jungefeldt, a famous Airedale breeder became interested in Shih Tzu and bought a bitch, Bjorneholms Pippi, from the now well-established Bjorneholms kennel in Denmark, owned by Miss Astrid Jeppesen. Miss Jeppesen had purchased her foundation bitch, Mai Long Tzu au Dux from the Kauffmans in Norway. Three years later, Mrs. Jungefeldt visited England and made arrangements to exchange her Swedish-bred Jungfaltets Jung Ming for the English-bred Fu Ling of Clystvale. Fu Ling was to become an influential stud in Sweden, siring more than 25 CC winners and was responsible for introducing the resulting genes of the Pekingese cross into Sweden and improving the early stock in both Scandinavia and England.

It was the Shih Tzu bitch Jungfaltets Jung Wu that completed her French championship by Ingrid Colwell in France, accompanied her to America and became one of the foundation bitches of the Si-Kiang Shih Tzu in the United States.

The Shih Tzu Arrives in the Netherlands

The leading Dutch fancier and breeder of Shih Tzu in the 1960s was Miss Eta Pauptit. Before embarking on a fairly extensive breeding program she made a comprehensive study of the breed in Britain and the Scandinavian countries. This advance preparation apparently paid off, for it wasn't long before her illustrious Oranje Manege kennels in the Netherlands became world-renowned. She bred many winners and future producers. One of her most famous stud dogs was the International and Dutch Ch. Hang Shu v.d Oranje Manege.

The Shih Tzu Arrives in Canada

A Miss Torrible of Victoria, British Columbia, imported a pair of Shih Tzu to Canada directly from Shanghai. They were Dinkie and Taikoo of Kokonor and were of unknown pedigree. But that did not deter Miss Torrible. She promptly bred them and had a litter. Apparently, it was not too difficult in those early pioneer days of the Shih Tzu to have them accepted by the Canadian Kennel Club. Its director for the Province of British Columbia, Mr. William Pym, inspected the offspring and pronounced them purebreds. They were entered in the Canadian Kennel Club Stud Book as Lhassa Terriers.

Another early Canadian breeder, Mr. Patrick Morgan of Murray Bay, Quebec, imported a fawn-colored foundation bitch, Hooza, from Peking and a pepper and white dog, Mingk, from Czechoslovakia. Both were registered as "pedigree unknown," but it was a linebred offspring of these two, Tashi of Chouette, a brindle and white bitch exported to Britain in 1935 that became the dam of England's first champion, Lady Brownrigg's Ch. Ta Chi of Taishan.

Miss Torrible continued to breed and exhibit on the Canadian West coast on a limited scale, but all the Tibetan breeds or "lion dogs" being shown at that time were registered as Lhassa Terriers. During the second World War they disappeared almost entirely and did not surface again until the early 1950s. This time they were registered as Lhasa Apso, and that is what they really were.

According to an article published in *The Canadian Dog Fancier,* the first dog to be officially recognized as a Shih Tzu, was a brindle and white dog, King Chan of Clarebrand, imported from England in 1958. His breeding combined two of England's best known kennels of the time, Lhakang and Elfann. We know little about his contribution to the breed in Canada, but we do know, at this writing, that a great deal of intelligent breeding is taking place in Canada at this time and Canadian-bred Shih Tzu need not take second place to any in America or in other countries of the world.

Shih Tzu are shown in Canada in the Non-Sporting Group.

Chumulari Trari, one of Si-Kiang Tashi's get, is here depicted at 10 months of age by the famous photographer Tauskey. She sits like a little gold, black-masked Buddah in front of the Easton's ivy covered porch at Woodridge, New Jersey. She became one of the Easton's foundation bitches and was the dam of seven champions.

3

The Shih Tzu in the United States

MEMBERS OF THE ARMED FORCES stationed in England during the war became intrigued with the shaggy little dog they found there and brought some back with them, introducing them into the United States of America. Others followed but, because they were not recognized by the American Kennel Club they could not be registered as purebreds nor could they be shown at American Kennel Club approved shows.

Because of this, some of them were registered, shown and bred as Lhasa Apsos, and today the names of Shih Tzu can be found in the pedigrees of many of the early Lhasa Apsos in this country.

This minor infusion of Shih Tzu genes into those of the Lhasa Apso seems to have inflicted no permanent damage on the breed. What it did result in was the Shih Tzu getting off to a poor start and was undoubtedly partly responsible for delaying their official day of recognition.

The second stumbling block for the Shih Tzu breed was the admitted Pekingese cross carried out by Mrs. Evans in England in 1952. While third generation Shih Tzu from the Pekingese-Shih Tzu cross were permitted to be registered as such in England, the American Kennel Club required another three generations to lapse before it would consider the Shih Tzu a purebred dog.

And, although still not a familiar breed to the general public, the Shih Tzu received some small degree of status in 1955. A group of active pioneer breeders were able to offer the American Kennel Club categorical proof that a substantial and sustained nationwide interest and activity in the breed existed in the United States, and it accepted the Shih Tzu officially as one of the 13 breeds that could be shown at that time in miscellaneous class, when such classes were offered at all-breed shows. As such "second rate" members of the dog fancy, they were permitted to compete in obedience trials and could earn obedience titles, but in conformation they were not eligible for championship points. Even purple ribbons were denied them. First through fourth placement for dogs and bitches is the most they could win and ribbon colors were similar to those awarded at AKC approved Match Shows, even though exhibitors paid the same amount to enter shows and obeyed all AKC and individual kennel club rules.

Over the years many breeds shown in miscellaneous class eventually gained official approval. Some fell by the wayside but not the Silky Terrier. It got its nod in 1959 and the Australian Terrier, after a long and vigorous fight, achieved recognition in 1960 along with Rhodesian Ridgebacks and Vizslas. But no breed in the history of the AKC has gained favor as quickly as the Shih Tzu from its introduction into miscellaneous class to that all-important first day of official recognition.

By 1960, two active Shih Tzu Clubs and a third faction, each with its own stud book, were limping along. These were the Texas Shih Tzu Society, The Shih Tzu Club of America, and Mr. Curtis.* At the 1962 Westminster Kennel Club show the Shih Tzu Club of America met and started merger overtures toward the Texas Shih Tzu Society. This was followed by a second meeting at Chicago International in April, where Jack Woods was selected to go to Texas and try to work out details of a merger. Finally, after considerable arguing and juggling for position, the American Shih Tzu Club was formed, and the stud books of the two clubs were combined. From that time on everything was UP!

*Mr. Curtis never joined the merger, but waited until the American Kennel Club recognized the breed, and then registered his stock with AKC.

The American Shih Tzu Club approached the American Kennel Club at every opportunity, and complied with all AKC requests in the long battle for recognition.

The American Shih Tzu Club and Its Stud Book

The American Shih Tzu Club was formed in 1963, and a foundation stock register or stud book was maintained according to American Kennel Club rules.

The first officers of the club were: President, Mr. William Kibler, Vice-President, Mr. Karl Thomsen, Secretary, Mr. B.E. Dudgeon, Treasurer, Mrs. Dorothy Gagnon, Director and AKC Liaison, Mr. G.F. Houston.

The first registrar was Lucien J. Duval, and his task was a formidable one. During that first year, 369 Shih Tzu were registered in *Volume 1, No. 1*, a totally fascinating hand-typed record of 24 legal-size pages, now dog-eared and yellowed with age. It listed the dogs alphabetically, with their sex, American Shih Tzu Club registration number, date of birth, their color, name of sire, dam, owner and breeder. These names were then cross-indexed, beginning with the first Shih Tzu to be registered, No. 001, a white and black dog English import named Yae Pae of Telota. This latter listing noted the origin and, if it was England, gave the number of generations that the dog was removed from the original Pekingese cross. Yae Pae of Telota was six generations removed. When possible, extended pedigrees of sire and dam were also filed with the Registrar.

A typical alphabetical listing was as follows:

Bjorneholms Tja-Ha (Denmark) (D) 226 10-17-19 WHGR
Sire: Ch. Bjorneholms Wu Ling ⊕
Dam: Ch. Bjorneholms Narbu ⊕
Owner: I. Colwell
Breeder: A. Jeppesen

⊕This sign, one that can be made on the average typewriter, meant that an extended pedigree of the Shih Tzu was on file.

At the back of the book, this same dog was listed numerically under No. 226.

The last three pages of the document was a kennel listing of breeders with their addresses and kennel prefixes, and a listing of the owners of foreign kennel names of Shih Tzu, imported and registered with the ASTC.

Shortly before the breed's acceptance in the Miscellaneous Class, Mr. Phillip Price, first President of the Shih Tzu Club of America, imported a little bitch named Ho-Lai Shum of Yram, and on January, 1957, she produced a litter of two puppies. These became the first Shih Tzu known to be bred and born in the United States.

The first recorded public appearance of the Shih Tzu was in 1957 at the Kennel Club of Philadelphia show. Here the Prices showed three of their Shih Tzu. Most Shih Tzu exhibitors wisely avoided the prestigious Westminster Kennel Club show in New York at this time, where Australian Terrier breeders and exhibitors were also fighting for recognition. Here the Aussies congregated in extraordinary numbers for bench display, exhibition and competition in the Miscellaneous Class.

35

The lovely Ch. Lakoya Princess Tanya Shu, pictured at ten years of age. She was owned by the late Jean Gadsberry, founder of Bomshu Kennels in California and now lives with Betty Winters in Massachusetts.

"Baby Doll" won the Toy Group at Eugene, Oregon, on the first day of competition for championship points and completed her title 27 days later, making her the second Shih Tzu champion bitch in the country. She is the granddaughter of Int. Ch. Bjorneholms Pif and line bred to Pif's sire, the Great Int. Ch. Bjorneholms Wu-Ling. Both Tanya and her sire left their mark on the breed. Tanya is the dam of three champions and her sire, Ch. Sopon Von Tschomo Lungma sired 17 champions, making him one of the breed's all time top producers.

```
                          Nord. Ch. Bjorneholm's Tsemo
                  Int. Ch. Bjorneholm's Wu-Ling
                  |            Nord. Ch. Bjorneholm's Lulu
          Int., Am. Ch. Bjorneholm's Pif
                  |            Ch. Wang-Ling
                  Ranga Ling 60/456
                  |            Ch. Ang Lahmu
      Ch. Sopon Von Tschomo-Lungma (ASTC #2340)
                  |            Ch. Bjorneholm's Tu-Tu
                  Bjorneholm's Bhadro 220868
                  |  Bjorneholm's Fie
          Germ. Ch. Tang-La Von Tschomo-Lungma
                  |            Ch. Bjorneholm's Wu-Ling
                  Int. Ch. Bjorneholm's Ting A Ling
                  |            Ch. Bjorneholm's Bolette
CH. LAKOYA PRINCESS TANYA SHU
                  |            Nord. Ch. Bjorneholm's Tsemo
                  Int. Ch. Bjorneholm's Wu-Ling
                               Nord. Ch. Bjorneholm's Lulu
          Can. Ch. Beldam's Kanshung Ling
                               Ch. Wang-Ling
                  Beldam's Chibitang Thing
                               Int. Ch. Thing-E-Ling av Brogyllen
      Int. Ch. Happa Shu v.d. Oranje Manege (ASTC #2452/NHSB # 2990 36)
                               Ta-Fu of Lhakang
          Ch. Fu Ling of Clystvale
                               Elfann Fenling of Yram
                  Int. Ch. Jungfaltets Pi Tze
                               Int Ch. Bjorneholm's Wu-Ling
                  Fr. Ch. Jungfaltets Jung Wu-Pi
                               Int. Ch. Bjorneholm's Pippi
```

But in 1959, two Shih Tzu were brave enough to take a stand against 34 Australian Terriers and two Silkies. We don't know if either was "in the ribbons" but it would be doubtful against such overwhelming Aussie odds.

After Australian and Silky Terriers were given AKC's blessing and Shih Tzu fanciers began to get their act together, Westminster stopped offering Miscellaneous Classes at its shows! Shih Tzu continued, however, to dominate the Miscellaneous Class at such other important dog shows as the Kennel Club of Philadelphia, San Francisco's Golden Gate, and Chicago International. At International, Taramont Encore Chopsticks was Best Miscellaneous Dog in 1963, 1964, 1965, 1966 and again in 1968.

The First Match Show

On Saturday, June 27, 1964, the first Shih Tzu match show to take place in the United States was held on the spacious grounds of Ingrid Colwell's home in Middleton, Pennsylvania. The show was sponsored by the Penn-Ohio Shih Tzu Club and fifty Shih Tzu were present. Considering the fact that there were only about 400 Shih Tzu in the country at the time, it was a surprisingly large entry. Exhibitors came from seven different states and as far away as Colorado.

The classes were judged by Mrs. Eunice Clark of Hinckley, Ohio, and Ingrid Colwell served as Match Show Chairman. At that time she was president of the Shih Tzu Club of America.

Best adult was the all-black Si-Kiang Tashi, owned by Margaret Easton and bred by Ingrid Colwell. Best Opposite Sex was the Swedish import, French Ch. Jungfaltets Jung Wu, bred by Erna Jungefeldt and owned by Mrs. Colwell. Jung Wu was handled by Ann Anderson Hickok, currently Mrs. Warner of Dillsburg, Pennsylvania.

Both Tashi and Jung Wu were descendants of the Scandinavian Ch. Bjorneholm Wu-Ling, sire of Ch. Bjorneholm Pif and grandsire of Ch. Chumulari Ying Ying. According to Reverend Easton, Wu Ling was a grandson of Leidza, the only direct line from the Western world back to palace-bred Shih Tzu.

You'll hear a great deal more about these dogs, as they were destined to play the all-important role of pillars of the Shih Tzu breed in America and today it would be hard to find a pedigree where they are not somewhere in the background.

By this time the entire dog fancy was becoming aware of the handsome little dog from China. Shih Tzu appeared in fashion magazines known for their snob appeal. Pioneer breeders such as Ingrid Colwell, Pat Semones (now Durham) and Rev. and Mrs. Allan Easton, were busy promoting and exhibiting the breed, professional handlers and established breeders of other breeds were becoming captivated by their charm.

Mr. & Mrs. William Kibler established their Taramont line, Richard Paisley in Virginia began breeding Shih Tzu under the Paisley prefix and, in Dallas, William Mooney surrounded himself with the attractive new breed. Susie Fisher took Bermuda by storm with Mar-Del's Chow Mein and Norman Patton travelled from coast to coast making a name for Jack and Mary Wood's Mariljac Shih Tzu.

The Great Day Arrives

And finally the great day arrived. On March 16, 1969, the American Kennel Club opened its Stud Register to the Shih Tzu breed. It was a triumphant moment for Shih Tzu fanciers and one they had been waiting impatiently for for almost ten years. As of that moment, 3,000 Shih Tzu, registered with the American Shih Tzu Club (ASTC) became eligible for registration with the AKC as foundation stock in the United States.

But five long months still lay ahead before the Shih Tzu could compete for championship points at American Kennel Club dog shows. When that day arrived, it made record-breaking history in the dog world.

Shih Tzu exhibitors all through the country set out for their closest all-breed show, each anxious to win the breed's first purple ribbon, each hoping to become the first to finish an American Shih Tzu champion. Little did they know that one of their breed would win a BEST IN SHOW in the East and two others in different parts of the country would top the Toy Group.

On September 1, 1969, Chumulari Ying Ying, Bjorneholms Pif and Lakoya Princess Tanya Shu skyrocketed the Shih Tzu to fame on that first official day of recognition.

Can. Ch. Chumulari Ying Ying, 3 ½ years old, owned by Rev. and Mrs. D. Allan Easton of Wood-Ridge, New Jersey, was named Best in Show at the New Brunswick Kennel Club at Metuchen, New Jersey. Alva Rosenberg judged the breed and James W. Trullinger judged the little dog in both the Group and in the Best in Show lineup, putting him over a total entry of 970 dogs.

I was only one of the hundreds of spectators there that day who were caught up in the magic of the event. Whether Mr. Trullinger's decision was based solely on the dog's quality or whether it was partly sentiment for the breed, no one could deny that Ying Ying was not worthy of his win that day. He was in magnificent coat and moved with typical Shih Tzu drive and vigor.

In Bloomington, Illinois, Int. Ch. Bjorneholms Pif, Ying Ying's

, Chumulari Ying Ying went all the way to Best in Show on that triumphant first day of the breed's ognition. The judge was James Trullinger and the show was the New Brunswick Kennel Club at tuchen, New Jersey. Ying Ying had a brilliant show career under the guiding hand of John Marsh, d is, without a doubt, one of the most important contributors to our present day Shih Tzu.

Ch. Bjorneholms Pif, owned by Mary Wood and Norman L. Patton, was the breed's first American champion. He took his first points on the breed's first day of recognition by winning the Group at Corn Belt KC, Bloomington, Illinois under Mr. J.J. Duncan, and finished 13 days later with three 5-point major wins. Pif also distinguished himself as a sire with 16 champions by May 1971, an impressive record for any small dog.

BIS Ch. Mariljac Chatterbox, owned and campaigned by Norman Patton in 1972, bears a str resemblance to his illustrious sire, Ch. Bjorneholms Pif.

sire, owned by Mary Wood of Mariljac Kennels and Norman Patton, expertly handled by Norman, won the Toy Group at Corn Belt Kennel Club under J. J. Duncan, and in still another part of the country, at Eugene, Oregon, a Shih Tzu bitch, just a little over a year old, Lakoya Princess Tanya Shu, owned by Jean Gadsberry, was awarded Toy Group first by Dr. Harold Huggins. Tanya is a granddaughter of Bjorneholms Pif.

And so, on that very first day, we find three related generations of Shih Tzu winning the honors: Pif, his son, Ying Ying and his granddaughter Tanya.

Pif accumulated his total 15 championship points within 13 days, with three 5-point wins at Bloomington, Illinois, Lafayette and Logansport, Indiana, to become the breed's first American champion.

Already a champion in five European countries, he was imported from Denmark by Jack and Mary Woods in 1968, and handled by Norman Patton in the United States. Pif was not only the breed's first champion but tied for Top Producing Toy Sire in 1970.

Ch. Chumulari Hih-Hih, a daughter of Si-Kiang Tashi, Best at the historic first Match show, accumulated the necessary points in 13 days, to become the breed's first champion bitch. Ch. Lakoya Princess Tanya Shu, earned her championship in 27 days, making her the second champion Shih Tzu bitch.

In little more than a decade, the Shih Tzu catapulted from a relatively unknown breed to one of the most glamorous of all canine companions. From the first day of formal recognition, Shih Tzu have been winning Bests in Show and the hearts of the public all over the world.

Issues of *Pure-Bred Dogs—American Kennel Gazette*, covering the first year Shih Tzu were able to compete for championship points, offer some thought-provoking facts. It is interesting to note that of the 93 American and foreign-bred Shih Tzu completing their titles, more than half were sired by only 8 dogs, each of whom sired 3 or more champions. These dogs were:

Early Shih Tzu Sires	Champions-9/69–9/70
Ch. Bjorneholms Pif	13
Ch. Sopon Von Tscho Mo-Lungma	6
Ch. Mar Del's Chow Mein	6
(Taramont) Encore Chopsticks	5
Ch. Mar Del's Ring A Ding Ding	5
Tailfu Fu	4
Ching Yea of Lhakang	3
Si-Kiang's Tashi	3

And so we see, even back there in those early days of Shih Tzu development that QUALITY begets QUALITY.

Left to right: Ingrid Colwell with Fr. Ch. Jungfaltets Jung Wu and Yvette Duval with Fr. Ch. Pukedals Ding Dang, at a Paris show. Both Shih Tzu were born in 1958.

4

Pioneer Breeders and Some Great Early Shih Tzu

SHIH TZU HAVE COME A LONG WAY since their first "day in the sun." Yet it may be good to pause and give thought and thanks to those early breeders who worked diligently to establish the new breed in the United States.

We all know that new breeders come and old breeders go every year, but the best breeders endure, and their contribution to the breed is inestimable. One has only to thumb through early breed magazines to find those "flashes in the whelping box." These transients' contributions to the breed proved insignificant. The genes of the few mediocre dogs they bred soon diffused and quickly faded into the genetic structure of the breed as a whole, without doing much damage.

Those early breeders, who had the stamina to ride through difficult, discouraging times, who took the agonies and ecstacies of breeding in their stride, and concentrated and preserved the genes of those early Shih Tzu, merit our gratitude. Without them, the Shih Tzu of today would not hold the position of esteem and popularity it has justly earned.

Ingrid in France with Fr. Ch. Jungfaltets Jung Wu sitting on the arm of her chair. A large white rabbit, name unknown, sits on her knee.

Mr. and Mrs. C.O. Jungefeldt from whom Ingrid Colwell bought her first Shih Tzu bitch, the lovely gold and white Jungfaltets Jung Wu or "Kia," holding left to right: Scand. Ch. Jungfaltets Jung Li, litter sister to Jung Wu, Int. Ch. Bjorneholms Megg and Ch. Bjorneholms "Kartas."

Maureen Murdock (*Harmony*)

One of the earliest Shih Tzu breeders in the United States was Maureen Murdock, who was active in organizing the Shih Tzu Club of America in 1957, and served as its first Treasurer. At that time she was living in Philadelphia, where she established her Harmony line from Chasmu breeding stock. Many early exhibitors and breeders bought their first Shih Tzu from Maureen.

Ingrid Colwell (*Si-Kiang*)

Undoubtedly the best-known and most influential breeder in the early days of the Shih Tzu in North America was Swedish-born Ingrid Colwell, daughter of Ingrid Engstrom, who raised Shih Tzu in Sweden under the Pukedals prefix. One of Ingrid's favorite dogs belonged to her mother, a Swedish champion named Shepherds Si-Kiang. Si-Kiang was the prefix Ingrid would later adopt in America as her kennel name.

Ingrid was married to a United States Air Force Sergeant and in 1958, while they were stationed in Germany, she bought an outstanding gold and white Shih Tzu bitch, Jungfaltets Jung-Wu, known as "Kia" from Mrs. Jungfeldt. It was not until 1959, however, when Ingrid payed a visit to her mother in Sweden, that her real interest in the breed began. Meantime she and her husband met Lou and Yvette Duval, when they were on furlough in France, and a solid friendship between Ingrid and Yvette began. Ingrid returned to Germany from Sweden with Pukedals Do-That for herself and Pukedals Ding Dang for Yvette. She and Yvette showed Jungfaltets Jung-Wu and Pukedals Ding Dang to their championships in France.

In 1960, Ingrid returned to the United States bringing with her four Shih Tzu, which became the foundation stock of her famous Si-Kiang line. Later that same year, Ingrid imported another Shih Tzu bitch, Jungfaltets Wu-Pu, who was destined to leave a permanent mark on the breed in his country.

In the days when Westminster offered miscellaneous classes, Ingrid attended, often entering four or five Shih Tzu, and always decorating her bench attractively. Andy Hickock Warner, a close friend of Ingrid's recalls:

> I went with her once. The interesting crowds that gathered around the benches were always exciting. Because of Ingrid's deep love for her Shih Tzu and her great salesmanship, she kept people standing, listening and looking. She sold puppies, certainly, but more than that she sold charm and good will. Ingrid had stacks of papers on everything that was written about the breed at that time, and she handed it all out liberally. No one who ever came into contact with Ingrid ever went away without knowing something about the breed.

In 1964 Ingrid instigated the first all-Shih Tzu match and served

Mrs. L. Svensson, Swedish breeder, holds Stefangardens Jasmine and Stefangardens Jenn Ling as puppies. Born in 1961, Jenn Ling was one of the dogs imported by Ingrid after she settled in the States.

Stefangardens Jenn-Ling, a silver brindle dog was a beautiful mover.
He weighed about ten pounds.

Another handsome Jungfaltets Shih Tzu, was Ding Ling, born in 1959
and owned by Charles Gardner and Ingrid Colwell.

as its Match Show Chairman. It was held on the spacious, willow-shaded lawns of her home in Middleton, Pennsylvania, and was sponsored by the Penn Ohio Shih Tzu Club. There was an entry of 51 Shih Tzu, and the day was filled with enthusiasm and good sportsmanship from the start to the conclusion, when everyone gathered to show, observe, chat and enjoy the hot and cold buffet dishes prepared by Ingrid and her friend, Yvette Duval, who lived close by.

Si-Kiang's Tashi, bred by Ingrid and owned by Rev. and Mrs. Allan Easton, won Best in Match, and Ingrid's French Ch. Jungfaltets Jung-Wu won Best of Opposite Sex. Of the original nine members of the Board of Directors of the Penn-Ohio Shih Tzu Club, one is deceased and four are Shih Tzu judges today. These four pioneer breeders are: Jay Ammon, Lucy Cress, Sue Kauffman and Andy Hickok Warner.

Late in 1965 the second Penn-Ohio Shih Tzu match was again held at Ingrid's. It was judged by Audrey Fowler, who came from England expressly for the match, and Winifred Heckmann of Maryland. It was another tremendous success.

From the day the American Kennel Club allowed Shih Tzu to compete in Miscellaneous Classes, Ingrid, and many of the other pioneer breeders, never ceased promoting the breed, often traveling across country to exhibit at shows in Chicago, California and Texas.

Had it not been for the wholehearted enthusiasm of Ingrid Colwell and some other influential pioneers, Shih Tzu fanciers may have had to wait several years longer before AKC gave the breed recognition.

On January 18, 1968, tragedy struck. There was a fire in the apartment house where Ingrid was then living, and Ingrid died from smoke inhalation.

Present-day breeders owe everlasting thanks to this pretty, blonde lady from Sweden, who devoted so much time and energy to promote the breed in America. It seems so very unfair that she did not live to see the Shih Tzu who exploded the breed to fame on that first day of competition for championship points. Many early Shih Tzu champions had Si-Kiang in their immediate background.

In the author's opinion, it would seem appropriate for the American Shih Tzu Club to offer a breeder's perpetual trophy in Ingrid Colwell's honor. Her unselfish dedication to the breed and achievements within it should be gratefully remembered.

Ingrid was one of the first Presidents of the Shih Tzu Club of America.

Mary and Jack Wood (*Mariljac*)

Mary and Jack Wood were interested in breeding dogs as far back as 1943. In 1958 they capitulated to the Shih Tzu, and were able to obtain their first from England in 1959.

Thanks to Andy Hickok Warner, we have available to us the names of nine Shih Tzu which Ingrid Colwell imported into the United States. They have contributed their qualities to our present-day Shih Tzu. Look for them on your pedigrees. Indented beneath each name you will find their birth dates and color.

Name	Birthplace	Sire	Dam	Breeder
Bjorneholms Tja-Ha (Dog) (10/17/59—Sil/wh)	Denmark	Ch. Bjorneholms Wu Ling	Ch. Bjorneholms Narbu	A. Jeppesen
Inky Dinky (Si Kiang) (Dog) (9/18/59—Bl/wh)	France	Ch. Fu Chang of Chasmu	Pukedals Do-That	I. Colwell
Fr. Ch. Jungfaltets Jung-Wu (Bitch) (1/1/58—Go/wh)	Sweden	Ch. Fu-Ling of Clystvale	Int. Ch. Bjorneholms Pippi	E. Jungfeldt
Pukedals Do-That (Bitch) (12/5/58—Bl/wh)	Sweden	Ch. Fu-Ling of Clystvale	Ch. Shepherds Si Kiang	I. Engstrom
Pukedals Ai-Lan (Bitch) (1/1/61—Bl/wh)	Sweden	Full sister to Do-That and half sister to Jung-Wu		I. Engstrom
Stefangardens Jenn-Ling (Dog) (5/29/61—Silver)	Sweden	Ch. Bjorneholms Wu-Ling	Siao Mei Mei	L. Svenson
Jungfaltets Pi-Dhona (Bitch) (7/4/62—Go/wh)	Sweden	Bjorneholms Dhondup	Ch. Jungfaltets Jung-Wi-Pi	C.O. Jungefeldt
Jungfaltets Wu-Po (Dog) (—Go/wh)	Sweden	Lhipoiang	Ch. Jungfaltets Jung-Wi-Pi	C.O. Jungefeldt
*Ching Yea of Lhakang (Dog) (6/11/62—Bl/wh)	England	Elfann Fu-Ling of Lhakang	Ching-Yo of Elfann	L. Widdrington

*This dog was imported by Brenda Ostencio but acquired by Mrs. Colwell very shortly after.

After Jungfaltets Jung-Wu's death, Ingrid imported several new dogs from Sweden, including Ch. Min-My-Shih and Blumihol Yang.

Both Mr. and Mrs. Wood were instrumental in forming the present American Shih Tzu Club and Mary served as Registrar for the breed prior to AKC recognition.

After Mr. Wood's death, the Mariljac breeding program was continued by Mrs. Wood and Norman Patton.

Int. Ch. Bjorneholms Pif was undefeated in Europe when Mary arranged to bring him to the United States, where he continued his winning ways. On the first day Shih Tzu were eligible for championship points, Pif won the Toy Group at the Corn Belt Kennel Club. He gained his necessary 15 points and both majors in just 13 days, becoming the first American champion Shih Tzu.

As a sire, Pif earned the respect of all dog fanciers, and even today retains the incredible position of #8 all-time top producer. He did this by siring 18 champions at a time when the number of Shih Tzu and Shih Tzu breeders was limited. Pif is behind many of our top-winning Shih Tzu as he continues to pass his greatness on to our present generation.

Norman Patton (Dragonwyck)

After Mary Wood moved to Terre Haute, Indiana, Norman Patton continued to show and breed under the Mariljac prefix. At the same time he became a professional handler, and handled many of the top-winning Shih Tzu in the country, including Ch. Charing Cross Ching El Chang, top-winning male in the country in 1974. Norman also adopted the Dragonwyck prefix during this period and is still breeding and showing dogs with this name today. He is well-known among Shih Tzu fanciers as a Toy judge and a breeder of many champions including Group and Best in Show-winning Shih Tzu. Among them is the breed's all-time, top-winner, Ch. Dragonwyck The Great Gatsby. Leased by Robert Koeppel of New York City, "Gatsby" was handled throughout his long and illustrious career by Peggy Hogg, to whom he was given on retirement.

William and Joan Kibler (Taramont)

One of the most important contributors to Shih Tzu in America was Encore Chopsticks, a double great-grandson of Bjorneholms Wu Ling, sire of Ch. Bjorneholms Pif.

In 1960, when there were only about forty Shih Tzu in the entire country, Bill and Joan Kibler were able to buy a pair from military personnel returning from Europe. One was Encore Lovely Lady, a bitch from English stock; the other, a dog, La Mi Ting Ling, affectionately pegged "Tango," was Swedish bred, the result of a Jungfaltets half-brother-half-sister breeding.

50

Ch. Mariljac Maripet, sensational puppy bred by Mrs. Wood in 1972, won Best of Breed over Specials and Toy Group 1, at the age of 9 ½ months, under the expert guidance of Norman Patton. He is Number Nine of the list of all-time top-producing Shih Tzu dogs with 17 champion offspring to his credit.　　　　　*Petrulis*

Ch. Dragonwyck The Great Gatsby winning one of his many Bests in Show with Peggy Hogg. "Gatsby" is one of Ch. Chumulari Ying Ying's Best in Show sons out of Ch. Mariljac Lotus Blossom. He was bred by Norman Patton.

Int. Ch. Bjorneholm's Pif
Ch. Chumulari Ying Ying
Int. Ch. Tangra Von Tschomo-Lungma
CH DRAGONWYCK THE GREAT GATSBY
Ch. Mariljac Chatterbox
Ch. Mariljac Lotus Blossom
Ch. Mariljac Tinkertown Toi

51

Ch. Charing Cross Ching El Chang, handled by Norman Patton for Mr. and Mrs. T. Phillips. "Chang" was top-winning male Shih Tzu in 1974. He had to his credit, 7 all-breed Bests in Show, 28 Toy Group Firsts and 60 Bests of Breed. He also sired several BIS winners including Ch. Dragonwyck Miss-B-Havin. *Petrulis*

                            Greenmoss Yu Li Ching of Wyndtoi
                Shao Li of Lhakang
                          Eng. Ch. Soong of Lhakang
        Ch. Chang of Kandu
                          Regency Buck of Elfann
                Cusha of Lhakang
                          Tashi Misty
CH. CHARING CROSS CHING EL CHANG
                          Holmvallee Lao Yeh of Lhakang
                Ch. Ho Tai of Greenmoss
                        Golden Oriole of Lhakang
        Juling Miss-Chief
                        Buda Buda of Rawstock

Ch. Dragonwyck Miss-B-Havin, bred and shown by Norman Patton in 1974, winning the Toy Group under Mrs. Connie Bosold.
Petrulis

Four years later, Ch. Dragonwyck Miss-Tu-Fi-Ying, bred and shown by Norman Patton, earns her championship from the puppy classes. She is owned by Norman and Chip Constantini. Notice the change in breed type from Miss-B-Havin, shown in 1974. Here we see the breed gaining in leg and neck. *Petrulis*

Another two years and many champions later, Norman shows the elegant and more refined Ch. Dragonwyck Dragonfire, which he owned with Chip Constantini. It's fascinating and a little frightening to see how quickly breed type can change in just a few years.
Petrulis

53

(Taramont) Encore Chopsticks.

Ta Fu of Lhakang
— Ch. Fu Ling of Clystvale
Elfann Fenling of Yram
Jungfaltets Sing Ling
Int. Ch. Bjorneholm's Wu-Ling
Bjorneholm's Gill Sing
Bjorneholm's Fie
La Mi Ting Ling
Ta Fu of Lhakang
— Ch. Fu Ling of Clystvale
Elfann Fenling of Yram
Jungfaltets Mi San Li
Int. Ch. Bjorneholm's Wu-Ling
Bjorneholm's Misser
Bjorneholm's Dott
(TARAMONT'S) ENCORE CHOPSTICKS
Wen Shu of Lhakang
Hung Pao of Buddleton
Jasmine of Lhakang
Yue Kaang of Ilderton
Bimbo
Tessame Loo of Elfann
Mafu of Lhakang
Encore Lovely Lady
Kepong
Wong Ko
Golden Su
Ahso Deska
Golden Dragon
Golden Loo
Golden Salween

Wen Shu of Lhakang
Ch. Mao Mao of Lhakang
Ch. Shebo Tsemo of Lhakang
Chingling of Hungjao
Ch. Bjorneholm's Tsemo
Ch. Bjorneholm's Lu Lu
Int. Ch. Bjorneholm's Megg
Ch. Bjorneholm's Lu Lu
Wen Shu of Lhakang
Ch. Mao Mao of Lhakang
Ch. Shebo Tsemo of Lhakang
Chingling of Hungjao
Ch. Bjorneholm's Tsemo
Ch. Bjorneholm's Lu Lu
Bjorneholm's Ta Chi
Ch. Bjorneholm's Kotzu
Tee Ni Tim of Michelcombe
Golden Shi Shi
Tee Ni Tim of Michelcombe
Ling Sing of Wyndtoi
Ch. Pei Ho of Taishan
Li Tzu
Tee Ni Tim of Michelcombe
Golden Shi Shi
Shebo Schunde of Hungjao
Om Mani Pudni
Sui Yan
Om Mani Pudni
Sui Yan
Om Mani Pudni
Shebo Schunde of Hungjao
Om Mani Pudni

"Lovie" was, quite naturally, bred to "Tango" and on November 11, 1961, 5 puppies were born. These were probably that first cross of Swedish and English lines in the United States. One of the five puppies was "Choppie." All were named with the Encore prefix but they were not legally registered until the stud books of the three existing Shih Tzu clubs were combined and the American Shih Tzu Club was born.

Meanwhile the Kiblers tried to register Encore as a kennel name but AKC refused because it was not a coined word. They then came up with Taramont, which was subsequently registered, and all future puppies bred by Bill and Joan carried the Taramont prefix. Since "Choppie" was bred by them and became the foundation of Taramont Shih Tzu, they always refer to him as Taramont Encore Chopsticks.

(Taramont) Encore Chopsticks had a brilliant show career even though it was strictly in the Miscellaneous Class. Each year the American Shih Tzu Club designated a show as the "Specialty" and "Choppie" won for six consecutive years, defeating imported champions from seven countries. He also won the Miscellaneous Class for dogs at Chicago International in 1963, '64, '65, '66, and again in 1968.

When the breed was recognized in 1969, "Choppie" had been retired from the show ring, as had many of his offspring. Nevertheless, he was the sire of 14 champions, and many of the greats in the breed today are descended from him.

At the first AKC approved Specialty show held by the American Shih Tzu Club in 1973, both Best of Breed and Best of Opposite Sex were descended from "Choppie."

Our thanks to Joan Kibler for sending us his pedigree and I quote her, when I write, "May his great qualities continue to show in the generations of tomorrow."

Rev. and Mrs. D. Allan Easton (*Chumulari*)

Two other dedicated pioneer breeders who have given so generously of their time and talents to popularize the breed in America, are the Rev. D. Allan Easton and his wife, Margaret, affectionately known to her many friends as "Peggy."

Both have known the breed for more than thirty years, though they became acquainted with it in very different parts of the world. The Reverend lived for some years in Peking where he was Rector of both the Peking English-speaking Union Church and the German Lutheran Church. There he became familiar with the Imperial palaces where the Shih Tzu, as we know them today, were first bred and cherished. He saw the last two known specimens of the breed to leave the Chinese Capital. They had been bred by a local German resident, Alfred Koehn, and had been purchased by the British Consul in Peking.

The Reverend D. Allan and Peggy Easton with some of their Chumulari Shih Tzu at their home in Gardiner, New York. In the foreground is the great "Ying Ying" in a charming, casual attitude. Notice the Oriental expression on all the dogs' faces and the delightful little chrysanthemum-headed puppy on Peggy's lap.

They lived with him in the luxurious old British Embassy until the time of the communist occupation, when the two dogs left with their owner for Hong Kong.

Seven months later, Reverend Easton followed them and upon his return to his native Scotland in the early 1950s, he tried to buy a Shih Tzu, but failed.

At about this same time, Peggy, a registered nurse working in Scotland, travelled to Cork, Ireland, to visit her mother. It was there she saw her first Shih Tzu. They had been taken home to Ireland from China by Miss E.M. Hutchins. Four years later Peggy met and eventually married the Reverend.

After living a few years in a rural Scottish parish, where they raised Siamese cats, Pekingese, and Tibetan Terriers, the Reverend was called to New Jersey, where he served for many years as Rector of St. Paul's Episcopal Church in Wood-Ridge, New Jersey.

Neither the Reverend nor Peggy had forgotten their fascination with the shaggy little Oriental lion dog, known as the Shih Tzu, and in 1961, hearing of a breeder of these dogs in Pennsylvania, they were able to acquire their first Shih Tzu from Ingrid Colwell, the all-black Si-Kiang's Tashi. Then they imported two others from England and these, along with Tashi, played an important role in the development of the breed in America. The first imports were the all gold Wei-Honey Gold of Elfann and the black and white Jemima of Lhakang.

A little later, in 1966, they imported from West Germany, the gold and white Tangra v Tschomo Lungma, which at the time was a Swiss and Czechoslovakian champion and later became a Canadian Champion. A great-great-great grand-daughter of the palace-born Leidza, Tangra was in whelp when she crossed the Atlantic and a few weeks after her arrival, her son, Chumulari Ying Ying was born.

There cannot be a Shih Tzu breeder today who has not heard of Am., Can. Ch. Chumulari Ying Ying. He brought fame not only to the Shih Tzu breed, but well-earned recognition to his owners, the Eastons.

Since then, the Eastons have imported dogs from Germany and Holland and, by means of judicious breeding have developed a Chumulari "type," which is readily recognized in the show ring. Ying Ying's contribution to the breed has been tremendous, and his qualities will continue to live on in future generations. He is the sire of 29 American champions, including six BIS sons, each out of a different dam. They are:

Ch. Carrimount Ah-Chop-Chop a Best in Show winner not only in America but in Canada and Bermuda as well, out of Am., Can. Ch. Brownhill's Yolan of Greenmoss, Ch. Chumulari Li-Liang, out of Chumulari Dorje, Ch. Mariljac Maripet, out of Mariljac Cha Boom, Ch. Emperor's Thing-A-Ma-Ying, out of Ch. Mardel's Flutterby, Ch. Dra-

The Eastons' Wei-Honey Gold of Elfann, bred by Miss E.M. Evans, the English breeder who dared make the now famous or "infamous" Pekingese cross. Her sire was Mister Wu of Lhakang and her dam was Elfann Gold Leaf of Tawnyridge. *Gross*

Ch. Chumulari Hih-Hih with Richard Bauer handling, wins her last 5 points under breeder judge Anna Cowie on Saturday, September 27th at Suffolk County KC show, just 26 days after official recognition, setting the record for the first Shih Tzu bitch champion in the United States. Her first 5-point major came under Alva Rosenberg at New Brunswick on September 1, 1969, that historic first day.

gonwyck The Great Gatsby, out of Mariljac Lotus Blossom and Ch. Dynasty's Toi-Ying out of Jaisu-Ling-Ho-Pla-Toi O' Dynasty.

Gatsby is the all-time top winning Shih Tzu and Thing-A-Ma-Ying is tenth.

Margaret Edel (*Mar-Del*)

Another pioneer breeder who acquired her foundation stock from Ingrid Colwell and joined her in the battle for recognition was Margaret Edel of Millersville, Maryland.

As early as 1962, she became smitten with the relatively new breed in the United States, when she saw Shih Tzu being shown in the Miscellaneous Class at Westminster.

After the Westminster show she visited Ingrid at her home in Pennsylvania and purchased two bitches. She and Ingrid became friends and some time later, the Edels made another pilgrimage to Ingrid's to purchase a dog, who was to become the first American-bred Shih Tzu to gain a Bermudian championship. The dog was Berm., Am. Ch. Mar-Del's Chow Mein.

One of Margaret's first bitches from Ingrid, Mar-Del's Snow Pea, when bred to Chow Mein, produced the famous gold and white top-producer, Ch. Mar-Del's Ring-A-Ding-Ding. "Ringy" was Best in Show at the 1971 Hunterdon Hills KC show under judge Emma Stevens.

"Ringy" is the sire of the top-producer Ch. Paisley Ping Pong, multiple BIS winner, Ch. Kee Lee's Red Baron of Mar-Del's, multiple group winner, Ch. Abacus Brass Ring, and many other winning offspring.

Andy Hickok Warner (*Rosemar*)

Andy Hickok Warner, a breeder of Standard Poodles, met Ingrid Colwell shortly after she returned to Pennsylvania with her four foundation Shih Tzu. She was immediately attracted to the unique new breed because of its outgoing personality, soundness and gentle disposition.

Ingrid gave Andy her first Shih Tzu. Si Kiang's Not To Be, who lived for fifteen wonderful years. Immediately Andy joined the fun, good sportsmanship and friendly atmosphere that she found among exhibitors in the miscellaneous class. Here Andy worked hard with Ingrid and other early fanciers to obtain championship status for the breed.

She bred her first litter of Shih Tzu in February 1964, and has continued to breed on a limited scale. Her Ch. Rosemar Very Bismark, a particularly sound stud dog, was prepotent in reproducing a large dark eye which eliminated white around it where it existed, and six

Photograph of a painting of Am., Berm. Ch. Mar Del's Chow Mein at seven years by noted artist John Gomez de la Vegas, presented to Margaret Edel by her husband, who was also enchanted with the new charismatic breed, when he saw Ingrid Colwell's dazzling display at Westminster in 1962.

BIS Ch. Mar Del's Ring-A-Ding-Ding, #5 all-time top-producer and sire of #1 all-time top-producer, BIS Ch. Paisley Ping Pong, shown winning the Toy Group at Suffolk County KC in 1971 under Iris de la Torre Bueno. "Ringy" was handled by John Marsh.   *Klein*

evenly spaced incisors between the canines, an important structural aspect in maintaining a broad lower jaw.

Mrs. Warner, an AKC approved judge for Shih Tzu, is still able to recognize her breeding when she sees it in the show ring, because of balance and soundness in combination with a pretty face. She feels she contributed to the breed by improving mouths, which were once extremely undershot, by shortening noses with a higher placement on the muzzle, and in reducing size. She would like to see breeders understand and place more emphasis on soundness and work hard to eliminate structural faults from their breeding stock.

We are grateful to Andy Warner for allowing us to reproduce the rare pictures of the Jungefeldts, Ingrid Colwell and Yvette Duval, and Mrs. Svensson with some of their progenitors of the breed found elsewhere in this book.

Pat Semones Durham *(Pa-Sha* and *Si-Kiang)*

In 1964 Pat Semones went to visit Ingrid Colwell with the specific intention of buying a Shih Tzu puppy. After considerable discussion, she talked Ingrid into letting her have her choice between a black and white female or a bouncy five-month-old puppy for $100. and two puppies back. Pat selected the black puppy, Si-Kiang's Beatle Girl. From that time on she and Ingrid were very close friends.

Pat selected Pa-Sha for her kennel name and in the spring of 1965, bred Beatle Girl to Ingrid's new Swedish stud Jungfaltets Wu-Po. Three puppies were born. Pat kept Pa-Sha Me Fancy Pants, a stunning black and white dog, and a small bitch, while Ingrid took the other male.

On Christmas Eve of that same year, on the same day that Ingrid learned that her husband had been reported missing in action, Pat's marriage, which had been shaky for several months, came to a crashing end. Pat went to live and work with Ingrid.

There she learned much about the history, care, grooming and breeding of Shih Tzu and became dedicated to the breed. In May, 1965, when Ingrid was away visiting friends in Chicago, Jungfaltets Jung-Wu, Ingrid's beloved "Kia," died in Pat's arms. Soon after this heartbreak, Ingrid gave Pat her fourth Shih Tzu, Pa-Sha's Shana, a daughter of Wu-Po out of Si-Kiang's Mitzi. When Ingrid moved to Georgia in the fall of 1967, Pat remained in Pennsylvania, but their friendship continued. Pat's Si-Kiang's Minnie Mouse, who was visiting Ingrid, died with her in the tragic fire that took her life. The majority of the dogs survived. Jungfaltets Wu-Po, Jungfaltets Sing-Ling, Ching Yea of Lhakang and many of Ingrid's other Shih Tzu lived out their lives at the home of Pat Semones. . . .

Andy Hickok Warner holds her Ch. House of Wu Mai Mai, bred by Rae Eckes.

Si Kiang's Not To Be, given to Andy Hickok Warner by Ingrid Colwell in 1961. The little black and white dog was sired by Stefangardens Jenn Ling out of Pukedals Ai Lan. Notice the longer, lower set nose and the smaller eye of the early Shih Tzu.

Pakos Lindy Fu, another black and white offspring of Jenn Ling out of Jungfaltets Fu Wi, bred by Yvette Duval and owned by Andy Warner. Lindy was born in 1962.

62

Ch. Rosemar Very Bismark, bred by Andy Hickok Warner, was an exceptionally sound stud dog, who contributed this important quality to his offspring.

```
                                          Jungfaltets Sing Ling
                                  La Mi Ting Ling
                                          Jungfaltets Mi San Li
                          Encore Chopsticks (sil/wh)
                                          Yue Kaang of Ilderton
                                  Encore Lovely Lady
                                          Ahso Deska
                  Ch. Taramont Ah So Onions (go/wh)
                                          Lhipoiang
                                  Jungfaltets Wu Po
                                          Ch. Jungfaltets Jung Wu-Pi
                          Ch. Jin Chi of Shu Lin (blk/wh)
                                          Ching of Shu Lin
                                  Mei Mei Tu of Shu Lin
                                          Yang of Shu Lin
          CH. ROSEMAR VERY BISMARK
                                          Int. Ch. Bjorneholm's Wu Ling
                                  Stefangardens Jenn Ling
                                          Int. Ch. Siao Mei Mei
                          Pakos Wu Lung (go/wh)
                                          Ch. Fu Ling of Clystvale
                                  Jungfaltets Fu Wi
                                          Nagara Tzu I av Willehard
                  Rosemar Laff Mor (go/blk mask)
                                          Stefangardens Jenn Ling
                                  Si Kiang's Tashi
                                          Si Kiang's Mi Tzi
                          Chumulari of Rosemar (go/blk tpgs)
                                          Mister Wu of Lhakang
                                  Wei Honey of Elfann
                                          Elfann Gold Leaf of Tawnridge
```

Rosemar General Nuisance is a perfect example of the higher-set, shorter nose and dark, expressive eyes in a solid-colored Shih Tzu. These qualities were to become trademarks of the Rosemar line.

Ch. Si Kiang's Mayfair Geisha, bred by Ingrid Colwell and Andy Hickok Warner, was owned by Peter D'Auria and Pat Semones. Only 6½ pounds, and probably the smallest Shih Tzu ever to finish, she bears a striking resemblance to her granddam, Wei-Honey Gold of Elfann, imported by Rev. and Mrs. Easton from Denmark. She was handled by Barbara Wolferman.   *Shafer*

Ch. Dragonwyck The Great Gatsby, owned by Robert Koeppel and bred by Norman Patton, established a record as the top-winning male Shih Tzu of all time. A son of the first American BIS winner, Ch. Chumulari Ying Ying out of Ch. Mariljac Lotus Blossom, Gatsby won fame as a producer and a winner. He is shown here after being named BIS at Burlington, Iowa, receiving the warm admiration of BIS judge Gerda Maria Kennedy and handler Peggy Hogg. *Olson*

Ch. Lou Wan Casinova, winner of the American Shih Tzu Club Specialty and the sire of numerous champions. This influential sire traces back to some of the breed's most important producers and has carried their stamp to his own progeny. He is proudly owned by Wanda Gec. *Ashbey*

Ch. Lisel's Rock 'N Rye, owned by Lise M. Miller, showed his quality early on. Finishing from the Bred-by-Exhibitor class, he won his first points as a seven months old puppy. His triumphs during the title quest include four majors and a BB over champion competition.

Excellent movement is obvious—even under the hair! This is the BIS winning son of Ch. Paisley Ping Pong, Ch. Hullaballou J. Ray of Nanjo, out of Nanjo Miss Wiggles. This dog rates #6 among all-time top winners and was a multiple group winner before finishing his championship at only nine months old. He is owned by Jay and Linda Ballou and was bred by Joan Cowie.

Ch. Lakoya Princess Tanya Shu, a memorable winner in the annals of American breed history. This lovely granddaughter of Int. Ch. Bjorneholm's Pif won the Toy Group at Eugene, Oregon in September 1969—on the first day the breed was officially recognized as a distinct breed by the American Kennel Club.

Ch. Afshi's Gunther, owned by Joseph F. Joly, III and J. A. Torriello and bred by Marc Bowman and R. Charles, was campaigned for less than three years and achieved a record as the #2 top winning Shih Tzu dog of all time. He was campaigned by Dee Shepherd to a veritable galaxy of brilliant triumphs.

A charming quartet of Shih Tzu puppies owned and bred by Ramonita Whitney. They were sired by Jen-Mi's Louie Primavera out of Dolmar Hsu-Hsi-Ying-Ling. *Missy*

Peter D'Auria (*Mayfair*)

. . . One of them, however, the enchanting 6½ pound gold and white bitch, bred by Ingrid and Andy Hickok Warner, was acquired by Mayfair's Kennel Manager, Peter A. D'Auria, when she was one year old. She must have been just about three months at the time of the fire, for she was whelped on November 2, 1967. Peter named her Si Kiang's Mayfair Geisha. She quickly crawled into the hearts of the author of this book and her partner, Barbara Wolferman, who showed "Gay" to her championship in 1970.

A year later, in February, 1971, at the time of Westminster to be exact, Barbara presented Ann with an eight-week-old Shih Tzu puppy bred by Pat Semones, Si-Kiang's Barban Chee Chee. She was a combination of English and Scandinavian bloodlines and was, genetically, not far removed from some of Ingrid's foundation stock.

Ann and Barbara both felt they were too deeply involved in Yorkies to become significantly engrossed in Shih Tzu. However, they bred Chee Chee twice before she was spayed. As a result she is the dam of several champions and the granddam of many more. She is still in very good health at this writing and is "house mother" at Mayfair.

Mary Frothingham (*Carousel*)

Mary Frothingham will be remembered more as a pioneer Shih Tzu fancier and exhibitor than a breeder. She was the first person to own and show the new breed in New England, and exhibited in the Miscellaneous Class at the Eastern Dog Club show under Percy Roberts. She bought her original Chasmu stock purely for loving.

She imported her first Shih Tzu, HonKon-Lee of Chasmu, a gold, black-masked dog, in November, 1964 and enjoyed him so thoroughly she imported a second, Su Shih of Chasmu, a cream and gold bitch, in 1970. Others soon followed but, it was not until 1973, when Mary bought Chasmu Solo, that her interests turned to breeding on a small scale.

As this was being written she was working with a three-month old black-masked, gold puppy, Carousel's Lucifer, who goes back to Ch. Chasmu Solo, and has the "old Chasmu look." Mary explained that the original Shih Tzu bred by Mrs. Fowler, were quite undershot, giving them the upturned nose. They had large dark eyes and black pigment, and were by no means Toys. Their heads were large and they had the inscrutable expression of a Chinese gentleman. She further described them as having a fishtail movement, like a fish out of water, and were perfectly beautiful to watch running loose in a field of grass or snow. Their coats were practically indestructible and did not have to be kept in oil.

Si-Kiang's Barban Chee Chee won 11 of her championship points and both majors from the puppy classes. Then an unfortunate accident occurred and Chee Chee would never again put her tail up in the ring. Prematurely retired from showing, she ultimately demonstrated her worth as a producer.

```
                                    Tui-Tzu of Tinkertown
                        Tui-Tzu of Wyndtoi
                                    Tzu-Ling of Wyndtoi
            Elfann Fu-Ling of Lhakang (sil/wh)
                                    Wen-Shu of Lhakang
                        Ming Chu of Wyndtoi
                                    Lin-Da of Wyndtoi
Ching-Yea of Lhakang
                                    Ta-Fu of Lhakang
                        Yung Mang
                                    Shi Hwan
            Ching Yo of Lhakang
                                    Bimbo
                        Yu Lan of Elfann
                                    Shih Tip-See of Elfann
```

SI KIANG'S BARBAN CHEE CHEE (Blu/blk)
*Half-sister to Si Kiang's Tashi
†Grandsire of Ch. Chumulari Ying Ying

```
                                    †Int. Ch. Bjorneholm's Wu-Ling (go/wh)
                        Stefangardens Jenn Ling (plat)
                                    Saio-Mei-Mei
            *Si Kiang's Jenn Wu
                                    Int. Ch. Bjorneholm's Wu-Ling
                        Fr. Ch. Jungfaltets Jung-Wu (go/wh)
                                    Int. Ch. Bjorneholm's Pippi
Si Kiang's Snopy-Snop (sil)
                                    Lhipoiang
                        Jungfaltets Wu-Po (blk/wht)
                                    Jungfaltets Jung Wu-Pi (go/wh)
            Si Kiang's Changa (go/deep red)
                                    Jo-Wil Tzeun-Ne
                        Chrysanthemum of Green Isle (lt apricot)
                                    Jo-Wil Ming Hwan Tin Su
```

Carousel's Lucifer, a black-masked, gold puppy, whose ancestry goes back to Ch. Chasmu Solo, bred and owned by Mary Frothingham.

A typical Chasmu Shih Tzu puppy of the '50s, with its upturned nose, large, dark eyes in a large head and the inscrutable look of a Chinese gentleman. Picture courtesy Maureen Murdock.

Ch. Char-Nick's I Gotcha (left), winning the breed at Carroll KC 1973 under Mrs. Louis Baker, handled by owner-breeder Louis Sanfilippo. On this same exciting day, "Gotcha's" daughter, BIS Ch. Char-Nick Be Witching of Copa (right) won Best of Opposite Sex with Jean Lade handling. "Gotcha" is #6 on the list of all-time, top-producing Shih Tzu dogs. He sired 21 champions, including three Best in Show winners, and all of them a credit to Louis and Florence Sanfilippo's careful breeding for quality.

Ch. Char-Nick's Sesame of Sam Chu, R.O.M. pictured winning Best of Opposite Sex at Westminster Kennel Club Show in 1972 under Heywood Hartley. Louis Sanfilippo handling.

"The gold in Mrs. Fowler's Shih Tzu was clear and bright; not muddied like it is today by the introduction of black," continued Mary. They had their own special look, as did the Shih Tzu from each of the individual English kennels. You could tell who the breeder was just by looking at them."

Florence and Louis Sanfilippo (*Char-Nick*)

In 1967, when the Sanfilippos, currently living in Arizona, were in the East, they became interested in the Shih Tzu breed and were able to purchase two bitches from Ingrid Colwell. Si-Kiang's Prci-Phe (Precious) was for breeding, and a four-month-old puppy, Pakos Lotus Blossom, bred by Yvette Duval, was destined for the show ring. They became the foundation of the Char-Nick Shih Tzu. Both achieved R.O.M. status, and the Sanfilippo's have never had to go out of their kennel to purchase another Shih Tzu for 14 years!

Ch. Char-Nick's Sam Chu was the first of many homebred champions, all owner-handled by Louis, and Ch. Char-Nick's I Gotcha, R.O.M. is undoubtedly the most famous of them all. He had a spectacular show career, taking Winners Dog and Best of Winners for five points at Westminster in 1972 at ten months. He finished with three five-point majors in a total of five shows. Under Louis' guiding hand he went on to win the breed at many of the most prestigious shows in the country, including Westchester, The Progressive All-Toy show, Maryland Kennel Club, Boardwalk, Philadelphia, Bryn Mawr, Eastern Dog Club, Beverly Hills and Santa Barbara.

Louis and Florence feel that Gotcha was the best Shih Tzu they ever bred, and there can be no doubt that he contributed his qualities to his children, grandchildren and to future generations. He was sired by Char-Nick's Mr. Chan out of the Sanfilippos' original foundation bitch, Pako's Lotus Blossom, who was still living at 15 years of age.

When Gotcha was bred to Ch. Char-Nick's Sesame of Sam Chu, R.O.M. the results were nothing short of sensational. The litter produced five champions: BIS and BISS winner Ch. Char-Nick's Be Witching of Copa, BIS winner Ch. Nanjo's Oh Mai Gosh of Char-Nick, Group winning Ch. Char-Nick's Swinger of Copa, Am., Can. Ch. Char-Nick U Gotta Believe, and Group placing Ch. Char-Nick's Fantasy of Gunning. Try to top that one! Totally, Gotcha sired 21 champions, including three Best in Show winners out of Char-Nick dams.

Not only did Sesame produce two Best in Show winners, two of her progeny by Gotcha also produced two Best in Show winners—BIS Ch. Nanjo's Oh Mai Gosh of Char-Nick produced BIS and BISS Ch. Afshi's Gunther, #2, all-time, top-winning Shih Tzu, and Char-Nick's Getcha of Davanik produced BIS and BISS Ch. Davanik's Starduster.

One of Ch. Char-Nick's I Gotcha's grandsons is the BIS and BISS winning Ch. Afshi's Gunther, campaigned by Dee Shepherd to #2 all-time, top-winning Shih Tzu dog.

Pakos Lotus Blossom, by Fr. Ch. Pukedals Ding Dang out of Pakos Lindy Fu was bred by Yvette Duval. She was purchased by Florence and Louis Sanfilippo when just four month's old, and became the foundation bitch of the Char-Nick line. Picture courtesy Andy Hickok Warner.

Ch. Paisley Ping Pong, all-time, top-producing Shih Tzu in the history of the breed with 39 champions to his credit. Like so many top producers and prepotent stud dogs, Ping is the result of half-brother, half-sister breeding from a long line of uncontested quality. He is a triple great grandson of Jungfaltets Wu-Po out of Si-Kiang bitches. His sire was BIS Ch. Mar-Del's Ring-A-Ding-Ding, No. five all-time top producer, and his grandsire was Am/Berm. Can. Ch. Mar Del's Chow Mein.

The greatest show-winning Shih Tzu bitch in history. Am., Berm. Ch. Witch's Wood Yum Yum, owned by Dr. and Mrs. J. Wesley Edel, Secessionville Manor, James Island, Charleston, S.C. "Yum Yum" was handled throughout her spectacular career by John Murdock.

Dr. and Mrs. J. Wesley Edel (*Emperor*)

In 1973, Ch. Witch's Wood Yum Yum was top-winning Shih Tzu in the nation. She was also top-winning Toy dog and placed tenth among all breeds. Owned by Dr. and Mrs. J. Wesley Edels' Emperor Kennels, Yum Yum's record for the year was 18 Bests in Show, 55 Toy Group firsts and 29 additional Group placements. This record also earned Yum Yum the Quaker Oats Award for the dog winning the most Toy Groups in the calendar year. Her cumulative wins add up to a spectacular 41 Bests in Show, 136 Toy Group firsts, 236 Total Group placings and 257 Bests of Breed.

Mrs. Edel purchased Yum Yum from her breeder, Marilyn Gireau, in 1969 when she was just four months old. She completed her championship as a puppy before continuing on her show career which earned her the title of the greatest show-winning Shih Tzu bitch in history.

In 1974 Yum Yum was retired and on her fifth birthday gave birth to a litter of four lovely puppies by BIS Ch. Emperor's Quapaw Quarter Emp.

Yum Yum was not the only star at the Emperor's Kennels. She shared the spotlight with Aga Lynn's Water Chestnut, top-producing dam, all Toy breeds, in 1971, and with two Best in Show homebred dogs: BIS Ch. Emperor's Thing-A-Ma-Ying by BIS Ch. Chumulari Ying Ying out of Ch. Mar Del's Flutterby, a daughter of the great Int. Ch. Bjorneholms Pif, and BIS Ch. Emperor's All That Glitters.

The Edels bred or finished 41 champions, 21 of which became the backbone of the Emperor's line.

Joan Cowie (*Nanjo*)

Joan Cowie has been associated with dogs all her life, so it was not out of the ordinary for her to become smitten by Shih Tzu when she saw a picture of one in *Life* Magazine at about the time they were recognized by the American Kennel Club.

Her mother and father established Nanjo and registered the name in 1952. Anna, her mother, is well known in the fancy as a judge of Toys and Non-Sporting breeds and as a breeder of champion Pomeranians, which she owner handled. Today, Mrs. Cowie occasionally shows a Shih Tzu at local match shows.

One day in 1969, Anna arrived home with an adorable, eight-week-old Shih Tzu bitch, which they named Wu Mi Tu of Nanjo. About a year later, Joan purchased a champion dog, bred by Richard Paisley, from his first owner who was forced to give him up because of her poor health. As a result of her illness the dog was in poor condition when she brought him home but, in a few months Joan had him in such

A Ping grandson out of "Sweetie," Ch. Nanjo Hi-Hope of Joy-Ful-Li, carried forward the Nanjo tradition of quality. He is a top producer like his parents and grandparents. Both his sire and dam are R.O.M. and his grandsire "Ping" is the top producer of all time.   *Graham*

Ch. Nanjo Ah So Sweet Sum Wun completed her championship at Westminster 1971 by taking Winners Bitch under Heywood Hartley. She is the dam of six champions sired by Ch. Char-Nick's I Gotcha.

Ch. Char-Nick's Mr. Chit Chat, owned by Joan Cowie and sired by Ch. Paisley Ping Pong, inherited Ping's dark, expressive eyes in a sweet face. When Joan found that Nanjo bred to Char-Nick produced a happy blend of type and quality, she bred back and forth between the two lines.

"Ping's" latest champion son is Ch. Nanjo Avenger, who completed his championship at Boardwalk in 1980. There is an obvious family resemblance among all these Nanjo dogs.

Nanjo Divine Ms. Wing is double linebred to both "Ping" and De Vilbiss Wind Song, Joan Cowie's foundation bitch and the dam of Sweet Sum Wun.

BIS Ch. Hullaballou J. Ray of Nanjo, another Ping son bred by Joan Cowie, was out of Nanjo Miss Wiggles. He is owned by Jay and Linda Ballou and is No. six all-time, top-winning dog in the history of the breed, proving again that quality begets quality. He earned his championship points at 9 months, winning two Groups along the way, owner handled. His complete show record is: 4 all-breed BIS, 1 Specialty, 34 Group 1sts, 63 other group placings and 135 BBS. Notice the reach of front legs as he moves with an upright head-carriage, straight topline and perfect tail set.

Ch. House of Wu Hai U was Best in Show at Metro Mile Hi KC under E.W. Tipton, shown by his owner Max Kerfoot. For three consecutive years, Hai U was BB at the Southern California Shih Tzu Specialty.

Eckes

good coat that he became top winning Shih Tzu in 1971, in just half a year of competition. His name was Ch. Paisley Ping Pong. Ping remained in the top ten winning Shih Tzu list for another two years.

Although Ping did more than his share of winning, it is as a producer that he made breed history as all-time top-producer with 39 champion offspring to his credit. In 1978 he was both the sire and grandsire of #1 and #2 top-winning Shih Tzu.

In 1970 Joan purchased a Ping daughter, Ch. Nanjo Au-So-Sweet-Sum-Wun, out of De Vilbiss Wind Song and, shortly after Richard Paisley's death, she was able to acquire Wind Song. These two bitches, along with Ping became the foundation of Joan's breeding program.

In 1971, Sweet-Sum-Wun completed her championship at Westminster with the coveted Winners Bitch award. At the same time, Joan was looking around for a compatible stud to breed her to. There, at the same show she saw Ch. Char-Nick's I Gotcha. Joan liked what she saw in the dog and Sweetie and Gotcha were bred. They produced six champion offspring, which became the backbone of the Nanjo line. They were Ch. Char-Nick's High Time of Nanjo, Ch. Largyn Forget-Me-Not of Nanjo, Ch. Nanjo's Good as Gold, Ch. Nanjo Hi-Hope of Joy-Fu-Li, Ch. Nanjo Rag-A-Muffin and Ch. Nanjo Haiku Dragon Brat.

Many litters later, one puppy in particular caught Joan's eye the moment he was born, and she watched him grow into something very special. He was Ch. Hullaballou's J. Ray of Nanjo by Ch. Paisley Ping Pong out of Nanjo Miss Wiggles. Hullaballou is #6 all-time, top-winning Shih Tzu.

Joan does not like to show her dogs herself, but is still very active as a contemporary breeder and exhibitor. Most of her dogs today are double and triple line-bred to her top producers, Ping, Wind Song, and Sweet-Sum-Wun.

Rae Eckes (*House of Wu*)

In 1969, Mrs. Charles Eckes (Rae) was approved by the American Kennel Club to judge Maltese, a breed she had been showing and breeding for ten years. At the same time she switched her energies and loyalties to Shih Tzu and succeeded in buying her first Shih Tzu from an Afghan breeder in California. Rae had seen a picture of Ch. Shaadar's Yan-Kee Dollar in *Kennel Review,* and had fallen in love with him. She bought a daughter of his, Shaadar's Yan-kee Doll.

Rae finished Yan-kee Doll at 12 months of age and, owner-handled, succeeded in taking her all the way to a Best in Show before she was 14 months.

After this claim to fame and a few Group wins, Rae retired "Dollie" to the whelping box. Here she promptly produced a litter of four bitches; all became champions.

Rae Eckes, pioneer breeder, still active today, holds House of Wu Mimosa (right) at just six months of age. On her left is a little sister, House of Wu Tiz Tu. The photograph was taken at Corpus Christi Kennel Club show where Mimosa won her first major from the puppy class under Edd Bivin.

Eckes

BIS Ch. Shaadar's Yan-kee Doll, Rae Eckes' foundation bitch, bred by Mary Smithburn. "Dolly" finished before she was one year old and had a Best in Show at 14 months, owner-handled.

Shaadar's Happi Boi Sam, by Ch. Shaadar's Marquis de Midas out of Shaadar's Gum Chim Tai Tai, bred by Mary Smithburn and owned by Joyce Jeppesen. He is the sire of five champions, four of them out of Ch. House of Wu Mimosa. *Eckes*

Ch. House of Wu Mimosa, born 9/3/73 was out of Rae Eckes' foundation bitch, Ch. Shaadar's Yan-kee Doll by Ch. El Greco Soket Tuya. She completed her championship on November 3, 1974 and is herself the dam of three champions.

Naturally delighted with her first litter, Rae repeated the breeding, but this time the litter was premature and she lost them all. She never bred Yan-kee Doll again. Instead she bred one of her champion daughters, Ch. House of Wu Mimosa to Shaadar Happy Boi Sam, a handsome dog owned by Joyce Jeppesen, who was just not interested in showing.

Sam accumulated nine points and one major toward his championship in spite of his distaste for the showring, but went no further. Nevertheless he did himself proud as a producer and his breeding to Mimosa produced five puppies, four of which won their championships. They were: Ch. House of Wu Wing Wa, Ch. House of Wu Sam Ting, Ch. House of Wu Hai-U and Ch. House of Wu Pee Ping.

Of these, Hai-U, will always have special place in Rae's heart. After putting a major win and a Group on him, she sold him to Max Kerfoot, who didn't waste any time winning Best in Show at Metro Mile Hi Kennel Club.

Rae has only one or two litters a year. She breeds her bitches only twice, then has them spayed and finds good homes for them when they are only about four years old and can adjust readily to a new environment. As a result, Rae breeds on a limited scale and never houses more dogs than she can properly care for and condition for the show ring. When she goes to a show, she takes a few really good dogs with her and looks forward to the pleasure and satisfaction that come from showing fine homebreds.

Rae feels that breeders should breed for type and not for fad or fashion.

Foreign Kennel Names of Foundation Imports

Kennel Name	Owner	Country
Antarctica	Mr. & Mrs. K. Rawlings	England
Brabanta	Mrs. E.M. Brabant-Holbrook & Mrs. H.M. Harvey	England
Birrawin	Mrs. E.W. DeSteiger	Australia
Bjorneholms	Miss A. Jeppesen	Denmark
Chasmu	Mrs. A. Fowler	England
Davaar	Mrs. A.S. Hendersen	England
Domus	Miss E.K. Bennett	England
Elfann	Miss E.M. Evans	England
Ellingham	Lady Haggerston	England
Geltree	Mrs. Teele	Australia
Ilderton	Mrs. S. Collingwood	England
Jungfaltets	C.O. Jungefeldt	Sweden
Kashmoor	Mrs. John Ross	England
Kuire	Mrs. J.M. Johnson	England
Lhakang	Mrs. G.L. Widdrington	England
Marbil	Miss J.S. Oakley	England
Metropolitan	Mrs. J. Kersch	Canada
Myarlune	Mrs. M.H. Bailey	England
Pukedals	Mrs. I. Engstrom	Sweden
Shanreta	Mr. & Mrs. Smith	England
Snaefell	Mrs. A.L. Dadds	England
Stefangardens	Mrs. L. Svensson	Sweden
Tawnyridge	Mrs. M.E. Arnott	England
Telota	Mrs. C.B. Newson	England
Tinkerton	Phil Beeley	England
Tinkertown	Phil Beeley	England

BIS Ch. Chumulari Li Liang, one of Ch. Chumulari Ying Ying's Best in Show sons, bred by the Eastons, handled by Pat Tripp. Here Judge William Kendrick awards him BIS at Calgary. *Hodges & Associates.*

Am./Can. Ch. Chumulari Ying Ying and his young son Chumulari Ho-Ping, Best Toy Brace at Westminster in 1971. The judge was Mrs. Yan Paul, handler Roy Stevens. *Gilbert.*

5

Breeding On—The First Twelve Years

No OTHER DOG BREED has ever captured the hearts of the American public as quickly and as surely as has the Shih Tzu. At the time of its formal recognition as a purebred, it was the 120th breed and low dog in demand on the canine totem pole. As of this writing it is the 16th most sought-after breed in the United States. Its rise in popularity over the past twelve years has been truly dramatic.

Novice exhibitors, experienced breeders and pet owners were attracted to the Shih Tzu, caught up in the ground swell of its successful debut in the show ring, and bought it to exhibit, to breed and to love.

In the next few years, following acceptance in the regular classes, Shih Tzu were winning championships, placing in Groups and winning Bests in Show all over the country.

The American Shih Tzu Club had a healthy membership, was thriving and spawning affiliate clubs in every part of the United States. From September 1, 1969 to December 31, 1970, one hundred champions, both American-bred and imported, were recorded in *Pure-Bred Dogs—American Kennel Gazette*.

The popularity of the Shih Tzu increased at such a tremendous pace that many of the early breeders were justifiably concerned about its future well-being. Often when a breed achieves overwhelming popularity, it suffers in soundness, beauty and quality, losing ground rapidly in both physical and mental attributes.

Not so with the Shih Tzu. Breeders obviously were trying hard to breed out faults and breed in the characteristics called for in the Standard. They were developing a regal, arrogant dog that was basically sound in mind and in body.

Parent Club Specialty Shows

The First ASTC national Specialty Show at which championship points could be awarded was held in Portland, Oregon, on May 5th, 1973. It was hosted by the Mt. Hood Shih Tzu Club.

Francis Thornton judged a Sweepstakes entry of 37 and selected Jia Ren's Has-Kahn, owned by Elayne Brown for Best Puppy. Best of Opposite Sex to Best Puppy was won by Hai Du's Honey Bear, owned by Susan Hardwek and Linda Miller.

Mr. Fred Stein judged the regular classes which consisted of 34 dogs, 28 bitches and 11 specials. The winners were:

BOB—Ch. Long's Bedeviled Bedazzled (B) (Charles and Janet Long)
BOS—Ch. Bel Air Tigherson of Shang Tou (D) (Cathie Phillips)
WD and BW—Laineux Wun Hungh Loh (Eve Hanson and Sylvia Kelly)
WB—Bel Air Bali Hai (Quellen Atkinson)
Best Puppy—Chumulari Pao Mi (Stephanie MacLeod and Margaret Easton)
Stud Dog—Ch. Long's Chiny Chin Ah Chop Chop (Charles and Janet Long)
Brood Bitch—Ch. Long's Little Lick (Janet Long)
Brace—Ch. Long's Chiny Chin Ah Chop Chop and Ch. Long's Bedeviled Bedazzled (Charles and Janet Long)

From then on, each year the American Shih Tzu Club has held its national Specialty in different sections of the country, each hosted by an affiliate club, which holds its Specialty either the day before or the day after. Often these are back to back with one or more all-breed shows, making the national Specialty a fabulous long week-end of point shows and Sweepstakes, and attracting Club members and exhibitors from all over the United States and Canada.

Thanks to Gilbert Kahn we can list the winners of the ASTC National Specialty shows through 1981.

1974 Sweepstakes—Winemaker's Fire Bomb (D)
BOB—Ch. Char-Nick's Be-Wit-Ching of Copa (B)
BOS—Ch. Geodan's Ron Eric.
WD and BW—Winemaker's Pla-Boi
WB—Winemaker's Ming Toi of Lou Wan

84

1975 Sweepstakes—Marlboro's Ursus Teddi (D)
BOB—Ch. Dragonwyck The Great Gatsby (D)
BOS—Ch. Moonlighter So Sweet Sum Wun
WD and BW—Jaisu Ling Ho X-Rated of Lainee
WB—De Ray's Our Gal Pentara

1976 Sweepstakes—Hapi-Our's Swing on A Star O' Copa (D)
BOB—Ch. V.I.P. Confucious (D)
BOS—Ch. Gin Doc's Champagne Lady
WD and BW—Abacus Chairman of the Board
WB—Ramurka's Hokus Pocus

1977 Sweepstakes—Silvermist Shag
BOB—Ch. Lou Wan Casinova (D)
BOS—Ch. Jen-Mi Kis-Sing Kin of Ming Toi
WD and BW—Cabrand's Midnight Special
WB—Ah So Georgie Girl of Hsu Jih

1978 Sweepstakes—Bel Air Gamblin Man of Mei San (D)
BOB—Ch. Afshi's Gunther (D)
BOS—Ch. Erincroft Qu Ti Pi of Jazmin
WD and BW—Pati Charlie Chan of Lainee
WB—Di Visconti Choka Khan

1979 Sweepstakes—Rockee Vollee Velvetier (D)
BOB—Ch. Yingsu Johnie Reb (D)
BOS—Lou Wan Slate of Li Ming
WD and BW—Jazmin's Maxi Million
WB—Pen Sans Peaches N'Cream

1980 Sweepstakes—China Chimes Chinese Satin (B)
BOB—Ch. Jolei Chinese Checker (D)
BOS—Ch. Charjalong's Kiki Kidd
WD and BW—Ti-Gi's Hotter'n Blue Blazes
WB—Wenrick's Miss Tiffany Sou Yen

1981 Sweepstakes—Luken's Sand Pond Full of Fire
BOB—Ch. Luken's All Fired Up
BOS—Ch. Hodari Lord of the Rings
WD and BW—Ch'ang Ch'u Apollo
WB—Clarlen's Dragon Lady

By 1974 breeders had size fairly well stabilized and general conformation showed obvious improvement, as breeders aimed for quality
with vigorous selectivity. Unsuitable dogs were culled, neutered, and
eliminated from breeding programs. As a result many typey, well-
balanced, specimens with luxuriant coats were being seen in show rings
everywhere. Toplines leveled out, fronts became straighter, and the
majority of Shih Tzu retained their strong propelling rear action and
desirable Oriental expression.

Ch. Mar Del's U-Betcha, bred by Harry Edel, Jr., and proudly owned by Joe Cannon, is shown winning Best of Breed at Virginia KC under James Cavallaro in 1975. Born in 1972, Betcha was an early winner attracting public attention to the Shih Tzu. He was handled by Bobby Barlow. *Gilbert*

Betcha's Litter sister, a sensational puppy, owned by Sylvia Hilton, Ch. Hilton's Fortune Cookie, shows a remarkable similarity of type and coloration to her brother. She completed her championship points at one year of age and is the dam of Ch. Hilton Lollipop Lover. In this photo she is being presented with BB at Elm City 1973 under Edith Nash Hellerman. *Klein*

Ch. Si Kiang's Jenn Wu
Ch. Si Kiang's Jody's Tidbie Toodle
Si Kiang's Changa
Char Nick's Mr. Chan
Jungfaltets Wu-Po
Si Kiang's Prci/Phe
Si Kiang's Mi Tzi
Ch. Char Nick's I Gotcha
Ch. Fu Ling of Clystvale
Fr. Ch. Pukedal's Ding Dang
Ch. Shepherd's Si Kiang
Pakos Lotus Blossom
Stefangardens Jenn Ling
Pakos Lindy Fu
Jungfaltets Fu-Wi

CH. MAR-DEL'S U BETCHA

Lhipoiang
Jungfaltets Wu-Po
Jungfaltets Jung Wu-Pi
Am., Bda. Ch. Mar-Del's Chow Mein
Si Kiang's Bamsy Wamsy
Si Kiang's Mi Tzi
Pukedal's Ai-Lan
Ch. Mar-Del's Samantha
Chin Tao of Greenmoss
Bermyth No Bu Ko
Tsai T'Sing of Shanretta
Aagalynn's Three Rum Collins
Ching-Yea of Lhakang
Aagalynn's Yem Yem
Pakos Lola

Affiliate Club Specialties

In April, 1976, the first Specialty show of the affiliate club, The Shih Tzu Fanciers of Greater Miami was held in Florida in conjunction with the national Specialty. There were 187 dogs in competition with a total of 279 entries. Elfreda Evans judged dogs and intervariety was Mrs. Erna Jungefeldt judged bitches.

Winners Dog and Best of Winners went to Jaisu Ling Ho Chinese Junk, handled by Faye Wine and owned by Donna Fritts. Winners Bitch was Nanjo's Mystique, handled by Barbara Alderman and owned by Joan Cowie. Best of Breed was Ch. Winemaker's Plai Boi, handled by Faye Wine and owned by her and Carol McLister. Best of Opposite Sex went to Ch. House of Wu Mai Mai, owned and handled by Ann Hickok Warner.

By this time hundreds of kennel prefixes were in evidence. Some lasted for only a few years, then faded into oblivion; others surfaced but made little if any impact on the breed; still others have been breeding, improving and exhibiting for many, many years and because of these dedicated fanciers, Shih Tzu continued to gain in stature and popularity until today they are one of the top contenders for America's number one Toy dog.

Standing in the sidelines, watching the breed grow in stature and beauty, no one can deny that American breeders have done a truly remarkable job in developing uniformity within the breed, in improving type and eliminating or reducing many of the genetic defects the breed brought with it from England and the Scandinavian countries.

Although the Standard of Perfection, approved by the American Kennel Club in May, 1969, is thought by many to need revision, it has served its purpose well. The current Standard gives the breeder freedom to express his ideas and develop his personal type preferences within the Standard's broad but definite confines.

Mouths, once severely undershot are more normal, straight front legs have, in general, replaced the bowed legs of the Pekingese, ribcages are wider and deeper; noses are shorter and higher, set between dark expressive eyes. Rear angulation has improved, hocks are well let down and there is usually a sound, sturdy dog beneath that gleaming coat.

Continuity of type is evidenced in the following pictures of Mandarin Shih Tzu through four generations. This is only one example of the breeding expertise of many veteran Shih Tzu breeders. These people have meticulously preserved the qualities of outstanding Shih Tzu of the past, bringing their virtues into present generations while eliminating faults and improving overall quality.

BIS Ch. House of Wu Mai Mai, by Ch. Rosemar Very Bismark out of Ch. House of Wu Tiz Tu, bred by Rae Eckes and owned by Ann Hickok Warner, was Best Opposite Sex at the Shih Tzu Fanciers of Greater Miami Specialty show in April, 1976. "Mai Mai" appears to personify type as specified in the Standard, under *General Appearance*: "A distinctly arrogant carriage. The Shih Tzu is proud of bearing as befits his noble ancestry and walks with head well up and tail carried gaily over the back."

Ch. Mandarin's Royale Rhapsody, R.O.M. is flanked by two of her champion offspring. Left, Ch. Mandarin's Sassy Samantha; right, Ch. Mandarin's Oliver Twist. "Precious," a careful blending of Scandinavian and English lines, is the foundation of Ruth DiNicola's highly-successful Mandarin Shih Tzu.

Ch. Char-Nick's Spiffy Laree owned by Joe and Roberta Walton was bred by Sue and George Nelson. His sire was the famous Ch. Char-Nick's I Gotcha and his dam was Char-Nick's Sheika of Macada. He was No. 7 Shih Tzu (*Kennel Review* system), in 1979.

A pair of beauties from Ming Dynasty Kennels, Fu-Manchu and Bamboo Shoot pictured at six months. Sired by Ch. Jaisu Ling-Ho Chinese Junk out of Barbara's Ming Tu, they were bred and owned by Gloria Blackburn. "Shooter" shown by Emily Gunning, completed the points for his championship in just six shows at eleven months of age and, even though a puppy was entered in open class. "Manchu" earned back to back majors at eleven months and finished his championship at 13 months. He was shown exclusively by Jim Blackburn.

Am/Bmda Ch. Kayesett Indo Gold, owned and bred by J. Herbert Kaye. By Ch. Cabrand's Midnight Special out of Ch. Lilibet Golden Dawn, she completed her championship by going BW and BOS at the ASTC Miami Specialty at 13 months of age.

Ch. Sam Ting's Puying completed her championship with a 5-point major at Texas KC in Dallas. Sired by Ch. House of Wu Sam Ting out of Ch. Sam Tsus Marhia, she was bred by Sandy Lewis, but owned and handled by Roberta Bossard. She "cut her show teeth" at the Colorado Purebred Dog Fancy's Fun Match.

Van Sickle

91

Mandarin's Madrigal, at eleven months, bears a striking resemblance to his dam, "Precious." Bred by Ruth DiNicola and owned by Mrs. Philip J. Harney, he is the sire of five champions. His sire was Ch. Glen's Fina Lee.

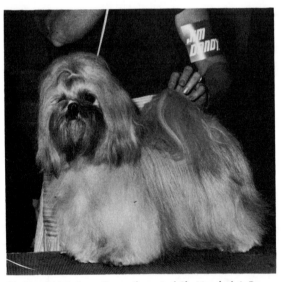

Ch. Mandarin's Sassy Samantha out of Ch. Mandarin's Royale Rhapsody by Am/Can Ch. Winemaker's Candiman, won the large open bitch class at the ASTC Specialty in 1976 under Elfreda Evans from England. "Sassy" is co-owned by Mrs. P. Harney and Ruth DiNicola.

Clare-Eduardo Studio

Shih Tzu Colors

A contemporary show ring filled with Shih Tzu presents a dazzling spectrum of colors, shadings, and markings. Gorgeous solids, golds, varying from deep bronze to the sheen and brilliance of sunshine, flashy black and whites, the brindles, parti-colors, silver and white, and charcoal. All are there.

Although the darker colors seem to be in vogue, the pastels and delicately muted shades have particular appeal and a beauty all their own. And, since all nuances of colors, all markings are acceptable, it seems foolish for exhibitors and handlers to dip into the dye pot to "enhance" the color of their dogs, to make forehead markings symmetrical, and darken ear fringes with mascara. The dye, usually quite obvious, detracts from the flower-like beauty of the Shih Tzu; the mascara, even more obvious to the touch, destroys the meltingly soft expression, giving the dog a hard appearance.

If the breeder wants an orange dog or a "red setter" red with white markings; if he wants a black mask and ear tips, he should breed for it. Successful Shih Tzu breeders have demonstrated their expertise in breeding for quality and soundness. Why not take it a step further and breed for color rather than lose one's integrity by stooping to deceit and subterfuge?

A breeder wishing to preserve pigment and distinctive markings may need to introduce darker markings or solid colors into his breeding program. Some colors have a tendency to fade over the generations unless depth is added to the gene bank. So, when selecting a mate, it is important to know that the deeper color being introduced is an honest one. The proof of the genetic pudding or the dye pot will express itself in the offspring, the sires and dams of tomorrow. There in the whelping box is the key to future generations.

Where Do We Go From Here?

Who will be the leaders in the years to come? Who will succeed in breeding quality and developing distinctive lines and who will fall by the wayside?

It is the dedicated, persevering, hard-working fanciers, breeding for show quality dogs, who hold the future of the Shih Tzu in their hands, not the casual exhibitor, the handler, or the pet breeder. It is the person who cares; who loves puppies and the breed and is willing to spend long hours watching, caring for, evaluating, selecting, training and guiding them through the critical periods to well-adjusted, well-socialized adulthood.

Another "Samantha" beauty, bred by Ruth DiNicola and Mrs. P. Harney, is Ch. Mandarin's Tantrum of Pinafore, sired by Mandarin's Royal Mr. Pinafore. He finished with three majors, including WD and BW at Golden Gate Shih Tzu Specialty in 1980 with John Brown handling. *Missy Yuhl*

Ch. Pinafore Mirage of Mandarin, also bred by Ruth DiNicola and co-owned with Mrs. P. Harney (handling), continues a progression of the "family tree." She was WB and BOS at Mt. Hood Shih Tzu Specialty in 1979, and is shown in a BB win under Wilma Hunter. She is out of Pinafore's Magic of Mandarin by Ch. Mingto of Greenmoss.

94

Ch. Mandarin's Royale Rhapsody, R.O.M. "Precious," handled by breeder-owner, Ruth Di Nicola is pictured with two of her offspring winning the brood bitch class at the 1976 ASTC Specialty under Elfreda Evans, the English breeder who dared to make the Pekingese cross. "Precious," is the only Shih Tzu to win the Brood Bitch class for two consecutive years. The offspring are from left to right Ch. Mandarin's Mischief Maker and Ch. Mandarin's Sassy Samantha.

It is the person, free of prejudice, who is able to appreciate the quality of another breeder's dogs; the person with a knowledge of pedigrees and the ability to analyze them and understand what trash or treasure lies within. It is the person who understands Mendel's Laws of Heredity and knows the importance of linebreeding; is not afraid to outcross when outcrossing becomes necessary or to take the inevitable gambles associated with inbreeding. It is the person who understands structure and movement, who has a deep seated instinct for type and an "eye" for a good dog. It takes a lot, but those who have it can turn dreams into reality.

Registry of Merit

Shih Tzu breeders should be grateful that they have a strong Parent Club with dedicated, progressive leaders ready to help when help is needed; ready to guide and advise without pettiness or prejudice.

In 1978 the officers resolved to compile a Registry of Merit, listing in its Club magazine, any sire who has produced six or more American champions and any dam who has produced four or more American champions. Shih Tzu achieving this goal are honored as top producing sires and dams with an ASTC Certificate of Merit.

Since September 1, 1969 to the end of December, 1981 48 dogs and 51 bitches have become "super-star" producers in the breed and have earned the right to add to their registered name the initials R.O.M. for Registry of Merit.

It is not possible to include the names of all the Shih Tzu occupying a place of honor in breed history but, thanks to Lise M. Miller, we present the all-time top-producers. These leading dogs and bitches, with the total number of their champion offspring, as published in *Pure-Bred Dogs—American Kennel Gazette*, and the names of their sires, dams and breeders are a further source of pride to all Shih Tzu fans.

Any such record can be misleading without an evaluation of the percentage of high-quality pups or champion-quality dogs produced in relation to the total number of offspring produced. Only the breeder knows the true genetic worth of his Shih Tzu and its prepotency in contributing quality and soundness to future generations.

Top Producers

Statistics for all-time, top-producing Shih Tzu dogs and bitches are based on the number of offspring as published in *Pure-Bred Dogs—American Kennel Gazettes* from January, 1970, through December, 1981. They were carefully compiled by Lise M. Miller.

Continuity of type and close family resemblance are
obvious in these related "super-star" producers.

Both the sire, Ch. Samchi's Vhima, R.O.M., and dam, Ch. Lansu Magnolia Time, R.O.M., of Best
in Specialty Show winner, Ch. Jaisu Ling-Ho X-Rated of Lainee, R.O.M. are Registry of Merit
Shih Tzu. Born in January, 1974, he was bred by Carol Walsh and Jay Ammon and is owned by
Elaine Meltzer. "Ling-Ho" was Top Producer (*Shih Tzu Reporter* system) for 1977–1979. He
was also a sensational show dog, finishing his championship in 13 days from start to finish.
During that period he had two five-point Specialty wins, including the ASTC under Mrs. J.E.
Clark.

Ling-Ho's daughter, Ch. Lainee
X-tra Amorous, born May, 1975,
bears a striking resemblance to
her sire, and like him, was a
Specialty point winner. Her dam
was Ch. Heavenly Dynasty's
Olivia, R.O.M. She was bred by
Elaine Meltzer and owned by
Pat Gresham.

Ch. Ming Toi Let'em Talk of Yen Von, a son of Ch. Jaisu Ling Ho X-Rated of Lainee, showed his siring potential early. At the young age of two, he had five pointed get in the show ring. He is out of Ch. Ming Toi Miste Jan-Yuh, and was bred and is owned by Yvonne Carey.

Ch. Ming Toi Bab-Ling Babs, R.O.M., born August, 1976, also sired by Ling-Ho out of Ming Toi Miste Jan-Yuh, carries on the family resemblance. He was bred by Judith Boyles and owned by Judith and Elaine Meltzer.

98

Top-Producing Shih Tzu Dogs	No. Champion Get
1. Ch. Paisley Ping Pong	40
2. Ch. Chumulari Ying Ying	29
3. Ch. Long's Chiney Chin Ah Chop Chop	27
4. Ch. Dragonwyck The Great Gatsby	26
5. Ch. Mar-Del's Ring-A-Ding-Ding	22
6. Ch. Char-Nick's I Gotcha	21
7. Ch. Parquin's Pretty Boy Floyd*	19
Ch. Lainee Sigmund Floyd	19
8. Ch. Bjorneholms Pif	18
9. Ch. Mariljac Maripet	17
Ch. Sopon Von Tschomo Lungma	17
10. Ch. Lou-Wan Casinova	16
Ch. Mardel's Chow Mein	16

*Ch. Parquin's Pretty Boy Floyd is the sire of Ch. Lainee Sigmund Floyd

Top-Producing Shih Tzu Bitches	No. Champion Progeny
1. Ch. Long's Little Lick	10
Dutch Ch. Tzi Klein V. Osterling	10
2. Mariljac Tinker Town Toy	9
Ch. Aagalyn's Water Chestnut	9
3. Chumulari Trari	7
Din-Ho Wang Shih Poppy	7
Ch. Dun-Kee-Wang Socket Tu Yu	7
Ch. Imperial Ping Tan	7
Dun-Kee-Wang de Kleine Osterling	7
Cooper's Sokatina	7
4. Ch. Nanjo's Ah So Sweet Sum Wun	6
Ch. Char-Nick Sesame of Sam Shu	6
Tai-Tai of Shang T'Ou	6
Chumulari Hsiao Chu	6

American Kennel Names

The following kennel names are most likely to be found in a modern pedigree. An asterisk preceding the name indicates that the breeder was one of the pioneers of the breed in America.

The author has tried to be as careful as possible in compiling the names, but there are bound to be errors and omissions. If possible, corrections will be made in future editions.

AAGALYNN (Gordon Kellogg)
ABACUS (J.O. Basil & R.D. Smith)

A rare head study of Ch. Paisley Ping Pong, R.O.M. number ONE all-time, top-producing Shih Tzu dog, owned by Joan Cowie.

```
                              Lhipoiang
                         Jungfaltets Wu-Po
                              |        ┌Jungfaltets Jung Wu-Pi (go/wh)
              Am., Bda. Ch. Ch.│Mar-Del's Chow Mein (blk/wh)
                              |        Si Kiang's Bamsy Wamsy
                          ┌Si Kiang's Mi Tzi
                          |   |        Pukedal's Ai-Lan
          Ch. Mar-Del's Ring-A-Ding-Ding (go/wh)
                          |   |        Lhipoiang
                          |Jungfaltets Wu-Po
                          |   |        ┌Jungfaltets Jung Wu-Pi
                     Mar-Del's Snow Pea
                          |   |        Stefangardens Jenn Ling
                          |Si Kiang's Madame Wu
                          |            Chee Chee of Kashmoor
CH. PAISLEY PING PONG
                          |            Lhipoiang
                          |Jungfaltets Wu-Po
                          |            └Jungfaltets Jung Wu-Pi
              Am., Bda. Ch. Mar-Del's Chow Mein
                          |            Si Kiang's Bamsy Wamsy
                          └Si Kiang's Mi Tzi
                                       Pukedal's Ai-Lan
          Ch. Paisley Petronella (sil/wh)
                                       La Mi Ja Jin
                          Kwan Yin Wu Tu of Sangchen (blk/wh)
                                       Myoshi of Shu Lin
                    Pitti-Sing of Sangchen
                                       La Mi Ting Ling
                          Ling Ling of Sangchen
                                       Metropolitan Merika (blk/wh)
```

Ch. Parquins Pretty Boy Floyd, R.O.M., number SEVEN All-Time, Top-Producing Shih Tzu dog. He was owned by Jay Ammon.

ALI-AJ (Terri Castellano)
BAMBOO (Diane Backovich)
BAMBU (Carolyn Terry)
BEEDOC (Bruna Stubblefield)
BEL AIR (Cathy Phillips)
*BILL-ORA (Mr. & Mrs. William Mooney)
BOMSHU (Dr. Clyde & Donna Steapp)
BON D'ART (Mr. & Mrs. Lennart Guggenheim)
BONZAI (Robin & Vince Gangi)
CABRAND (Catherine Gec)
CAROUSEL (Sandra Lucchu)
CARRIMOUNT (Mrs. Jeffrey Carrique)
CHARING CROSS (Gilbert Kahn & Jorge Sanchez)
CHARJALONG (Mr. & Mrs. Charles Long)
*CHAR-NICK (Mr. & Mrs. Louis Sanfilippo)
*CHUMULARI (Rev. and Mrs. D. Allan Easton)
CINNABAR (Carol Daniels)
*COLEMAN (Mr. & Mrs. Jack Coleman)
CON WYNN (Del & Connie Smart)
COPPER PENNY (Barbara Pennington)
DANDYLION (Gilbert Arnold)
DAVANIK (Peggy Angelastro)
DELRAY (Delores Snopek)
DING-A-LING (Sally Murphy)
DIN HO (Mrs. Howard Strom)
DRAGONWYCK (Norman Patton)
ELTRI (Mary Lou Ellis & Thomas Tripp)
*EMPEROR (Mr. & Mrs. Wesley Edel)
*ENCORE (Mrs. Jane Fitts)
FANCEE (Mrs. Marion "Dolly" Wheeler)
FANG CHU (Mr. & Mrs. John Hollingsworth)
FLORIDONNA (Ed & Donna Ellis)
*FOREMAN (Mrs. John Foreman)
FORESTFARM (Mary Frothingham)
*GAGNON (Mrs. Dorothy Gagnon)
*GAYWOOD (Jane Fitts)
*GOOD TIME (Mrs. Eloise Craig)
GUNNING (Mr. & Mrs. Sean Gunning)
HAI SING (Charles, Vera & La Mar Hayward)
HAPPI (Dan & Sue Archer)
*HARMONY (Miss Maureen Murdock)
*HASU (Mrs. Joyce Larson)
HEAVENLY DYNASTY (Jo Ann White)
HIGHLAND HOUSE (Carol Bognor)
HODARI (Laura Battey)
HONEYCOMB (Loyal & Sheila Lister)
*HOUSE OF WU (Mrs. Charles Eckes)
HSU-JOR (Linda Miller)
HULLABALLOU (Jay & Linda Ballou)
HY-TOR (Gilliam Wilson)
*JAISU (Sue Kaufman & Jay Ammon)
JASMIN (Mr. & Mrs. James Peterson)

JENNYLYN (Jennifer Winship)
JEN-MI (Sharon Heuser)
JOLEI (Ed, Arlys & Diane Kijowski)
*JONEDITH (Mrs. Edith Groves)
*JO-WIL (Mrs. J.D. Curtice)
*JUDLU (Mr. & Mrs. George Houston)
KATINKA (Mr. & Mrs. Joseph Edwards)
KUBLAI KHAN (Dr. D.G. Peace)
*KWAN YIN (Mrs. Brenda Ostencio)
LAINEE (Elaine Meltzer)
*LA-MI (Mr. & Mrs. Charles Gardner)
LI MING (Mr. & Mrs. Robert Tendler)
LISEL (Mr. & Mrs. Alan Miller)
*LOO WI (Mrs. Noel Alford)
LOUBRED (Louis & Brenda McKnight)
LOU WAN (Louis & Wanda Gec)
LUKEN (Jean & E.R. Luckenbach)
LUVUNCARE (Rosemarie Hoo)
MANDARIN (Ruth DiNicola)
*MARILJAC (Mrs. Mary Wood)
MEI SAN (Betty Meidlinger)
*MOGENE (Mr. & Mrs. Benton Dudgeon)
MYSTY DAI (Dorothy Poole)
*NANJO (Joan Cowie)
NANKING (Jerry Ikola)
NAT SAM'S (Al Marcum)
*OLINGER (Col. & Mrs. Robert Olinger)
*PAISLEY (Richard Paisley)
*PAKO (Yvette Duval)
*PASHA (Pat Semones Durham)
PEN SANS (Gloria Busselman)
PINAFORE (Mrs. Phillip J. Harney)
PINE HAVEN (Lucille & Nelson Huntsman)
REGAL (Mr. & Mrs. Joseph Regelman)
*REYNOLDS (Mr. & Mrs. Eugene Reynolds)
*ROSEMAR (Mrs. Andy Hickok Warner)
ROCKEE VOLLEE (Helen Mueller)
SAMSU (Michael & Debra Bush)
SAMURI (Donna Fritts or Cheryl Green)
SANCHI (Bonnie Selfon)
*SANGCHEN (Mrs. Pat Michaels)
SAN YEN (Susan Donleavy Barr)
SHA NEL'S (Sharon Nelson)
SHANG T'OU (Eleanore Eldredge)
SHEN WAY (Mr. & Mrs. Joe Walton)
*SHU LIN (Dr. & Mrs. Sidney Bashore)
*SI-KIANG (Ingrid Colwell)
*SILVER NYMPH (Mrs. Theresa Drimal)
*STONYACRES (Mrs. Thelma Ruth)
*STR-RANGE (Mr. Joe Strange)
*SURREY (Richard Bauer)
*TAMWORTH (Col. & Mrs. J. Lett)

104

*TARAMONT (Mr. & Mrs. William Kibler)
*TING CHIA (Philip N. Price)
TIPTON (Sharon & Ralf Heusen)
*TURN AGAIN LANE (Mrs. Patricia Michaels)
*VICHI (Vicki Pitts)
WEGMAN (Linda Wegman)
WENDAR (David Lehmann)
WENRICK (Mr. & Mrs. Richard Paquette)
WEN SHU (Mr. & Mrs. Floyd Gerl)
WESTWOOD MANOR (Gabriella Hoffman)
WIND CHANT (Valerie Peterson)
WINEMAKER (Faye Wine)
WIX TOI (Glenda Wicks)
WYLLSON (Betty Wilson)
YEN VON (Yvonne Carey)
YINGSU (Sue Miller)
ZANDU (Jack & Angie Zay)
*ZIJUH (Col. & Mrs. Frank Loob)

Ch. Beedoc the Floozy of Lainee, born November, 1976, another Elaine Meltzer bitch and specialty point winner, was bred by Bruna Stubblefield. She is by Ch. Parquin's Pretty Boy Floyd, R.O.M. out of Ch. Beedoc's Chuch Shib Mei Jen, R.O.M.

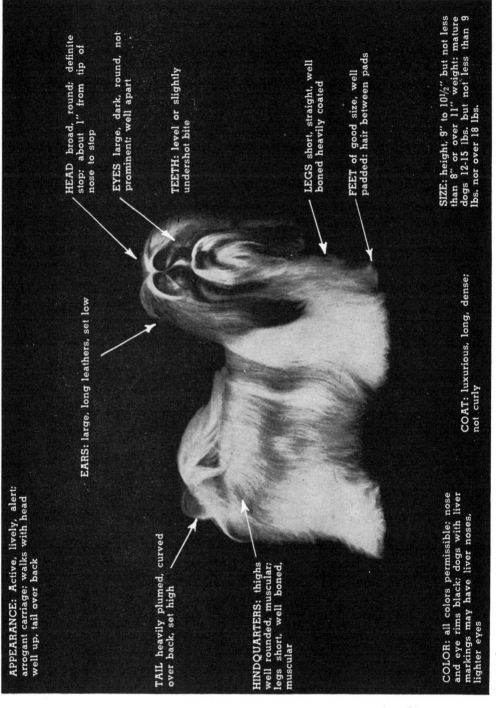

APPEARANCE: Active, lively, alert; arrogant carriage; walks with head well up; tail over back

EARS: large, long leathers, set low

TAIL heavily plumed, curved over back, set high

HINDQUARTERS: thighs well rounded, muscular; legs short, well boned, muscular

COLOR: all colors permissible; nose and eye rims black; dogs with liver markings may have liver noses, lighter eyes

HEAD broad, round; definite stop; about 1" from tip of nose to stop

EYES large, dark, round, not prominent; well apart

TEETH: level or slightly undershot bite

LEGS short, straight, well boned heavily coated

FEET of good size, well padded; hair between pads

COAT: luxurious, long, dense; not curly

SIZE: height, 9" to 10½" but not less than 8" or over 11" weight: mature dogs 12-15 lbs. but not less than 9 lbs. nor over 18 lbs.

SHIH TZU standard visualization.

6

The Shih Tzu Standard

LIKE EVERY OTHER DOG BREED, the Shih Tzu had to have a Standard of Perfection before it could be admitted into the American Kennel Club Studbook of purebreds.

Such a standard is generally compiled by men and women who have long been associated with the breed and are able to describe it so succinctly that a breeder, a judge or just someone on the periphery of the dog fancy—an artist or sculptor, for example—should be able to visualize the breed and distinguish it from others. The drafted standard is then submitted to the breed club membership for its approval before it is adopted by the club.

Generally breed type, structure and major characteristics are quite specific. On the other hand, most standards are purposely left broad enough to allow the breeder freedom to express his ideal within its framework, while still maintaining basic type and breed characteristics.

In many ways, a good breeder is an artist. He expresses himself in canine bone, muscle, flesh and blood in much the same way a sculptor chisels his marble or an artist builds his canvas. And like the sculptor or artist, the breeder should have a definite concept of what he wants to create to eventually approximate his ideal. The breeder should be able to go to the standard to formulate his mental portrait.

Too often, however, breeders and judges allow what is winning in the show ring to influence their judgement and set breed type in their minds. What a judge likes or has been told by another breeder is correct, is not necessarily what the standard specifies. It just happens to be what that particular breeder is producing at the moment.

Fads come and fads go, but quality carries on from one generation to the next, so breeders and judges must constantly turn back to the standard and let that be the only deciding factor in evaluating their breeding stock or the dogs in the show ring.

The First Standard

The Chinese Standard formulated in 1939 and included in Chapter 2 was merely an outline. It left a great deal to be desired. What is interesting is the span in weight from 10 to 15 pounds and an overall size from 9 to 12 inches high; 13 to 18 inches long.

Another point of interest is the apparent fact that, as early as 1939, the Chinese were working toward straight front legs. The original Chinese Shih Tzu, according to Audrey Fowler, were barrel-chested with bowed front legs.

The Chinese Standard was used as a stepping stone by the English Shih Tzu Club in 1939, when it devised a cursory standard, adequate to serve as a guideline by early breeders, but still permitting breed improvement and the development of type.

In 1948, after the war ended and the breed had developed more distinguishing characteristics and uniformity, a new Standard was formulated. It maintained that Shih Tzu are "not Toys." At the same time, the maximum size was specified at "about 11 inches at the withers,"* one inch smaller than the maximum allowed in the Chinese Standard. But it qualified this by adding, "considerable variation from this Standard is permissible, providing other proportions are correct and true to type." Length of body was specified as "considerably longer than height of withers." Front legs are described as "short, straight and muscular;" in 1953 the word "straight" was deleted, as the controversy over straight, bowed or slightly bowed continued. Bowed front legs predisposes a barrel-shaped chest.

English Breed Standard, 1948

Head—Broad, round, wide between the eyes; shock-headed with hair falling over the eyes; good beard and whiskers, the hair growing upwards on the nose, giving a distinctly chrysanthemum-like effect.

---

*The Lhasa Apso Standard, approved July 11, 1978, specifies size as variable, but about 10 or 11 inches at shoulder for dogs, bitches slightly smaller.

Eyes—Large, dark and round (by 1949 it was considered necessary to include "but not prominent")

Muzzle—Square, short, but not wrinkled like a Pekingese, flat and hairy.

Ears—Large, and carried drooping, so heavily coated that they appear to blend with the hair of the neck.

Body—Body between withers and root of tail should be considerably longer than height of withers, well ribbed up.

Legs—Short, straight and muscular, heavily coated, with feet big and hair between pads (*Note*—word straight, deleted in 1953)

Tail—Heavily coated and curled well over back, set on high.

Coat—Long and dense but not curly; looks harsher than it feels to the touch.

Colours—All colours, but a white blaze on the forehead and a white tip on the tail are highly prized.

Size—About 11 inches at the withers, but considerable variation from this standard is permissible, provided other proportions are correct and true to type.

General Appearance—Not Toys, very active, lively and alert, with a distinctly arrogant carriage.

Present British Standard

The present British Standard is more specific, but avoids the shape of the front legs, stating only they should be short and muscular with ample bone and the word, "considerable" in describing body length is omitted.

(The words in parentheses are the American equivalent for the English term shown and the italicized words and phrases are the parts of the English Standard omitted from the American Standard of 1969.)

General Appearance—Very active, lively and alert, with a distinctly arrogant carriage. *The Shih Tzu is neither a terrier nor a toy dog.*

Head and Skull—Head broad and round, wide between the eyes. *Shock-headed with hair falling over the eyes. Good beard and whiskers; the hair growing upwards on the nose gives a distinctly chrysanthemum-like effect.* Muzzle square and short, but not wrinkled *like a Pekingese*; flat and hairy. Nose black for preference and about one inch from tip to stop.

Ears—Large, with long leathers, and carried drooping. Set slightly below the crown of the skull; so heavily coated that they appear to blend with the hair of the neck.

Mouth—Level or slightly underhung (undershot)

Forequarters—Legs short and muscular with ample bone. The legs should look massive on account of the wealth of hair.

Body—Body between withers and root of tail should be longer than height at withers; well-coupled and sturdy; chest broad and deep, shoulders firm, back level.

Hindquarters—Legs short and muscular with ample bone. They should look straight when viewed from the rear. Thighs well rounded and muscular. Legs should look massive on account of the wealth of the hair.

Feet—Firm and well-padded. *They should look big on account of the wealth of the hair.*

Tail—Heavily plumed, *curled* (curved) well over back; carried gaily, set on high.

Coat—Long and dense, but not curly, with good undercoat.

Colours—All colours permissible, *but a white blaze on the forehead and a white tip to the tail are highly prized.* Dogs with liver markings have dark liver noses and slightly lighter eyes. *Pigmentation on muzzle as unbroken as possible.*

Weight and Size—*10–18 lbs., ideal weight 9–16 lbs. Height at withers, not more than 10 ½ in.* Type and breed characteristics of greatest importance *and on no account to be sacrificed to size alone.*

Faults—Narrow heads, pig jaws (overshot bite), snipiness, *pale*-pink noses and eye-rims, small or light eyes, legginess, sparse coat.

The British Standard was used as a model when the American Shih Tzu Club devised its Standard for the United States. In it, front legs again become "straight." It was approved by the Board of Directors of the American Kennel Club and became effective on September 1, 1969.

The Official Standard for the Shih Tzu in the United States

General Appearance—Very active, lively and alert, with a distinctly arrogant carriage. The Shih Tzu is proud of bearing as befits his noble ancestry, and walks with head well up and tail carried gaily over the back.

Head—Broad and round, wide between the eyes. Muzzle square and short, but not wrinkled, about one inch from tip of nose to stop. *Definite stop. Eyes*—Large, dark and round but not prominent, placed well apart. Eyes should show warm expression. *Ears*—Large, with long leathers, and carried drooping; set slightly below the crown of the skull; so heavily coated that they appear to blend with the hair of the neck. *Teeth*—Level or slightly undershot bite.

Forequarters—Legs short, straight, well boned, muscular, and heavily coated. Legs and feet look massive on account of the wealth of hair.

Body—Body between the withers and the root of the tail is somewhat longer than the height at the withers; well coupled and sturdy. Chest broad and deep, shoulders firm, back level.

Hindquarters—Legs short, well boned and muscular, are straight when viewed from the rear. Thighs well rounded and muscular. Legs look massive on account of wealth of hair.

Feet—Of good size, firm, well padded, with hair between the pads. Dewclaws, if any, on the hind legs are generally removed. Dewclaws on the forelegs may be removed.

Tail—Heavily plumed and curved well over the back, carried gaily, set on high.

Coat—A luxurious, long, dense coat. May be slightly wavy but *not* curly. The hair on top of the head may be tied up.

Color—All colors permissible. Nose and eye rims black, except that dogs with liver markings may have liver noses and slightly lighter eyes.

Gait—Slightly rolling, smooth and flowing, with strong rear action.

Size—Height at withers—9 to 10 ½ inches—should be no more than 11 inches nor less than 8 inches. Weight of mature dogs—12 to 15 pounds–should be no more than 18 nor less than 9 pounds. However, type and breed characteristics are of the greatest importance.

Faults

Narrow head, overshot bite, snippiness, pink on nose or eye rims, small or light eyes, legginess, sparse coat, lack of definite stop.

Approved May 13, 1969

The Standard adequately defines breed characteristics and type, but it leaves some soft spots such as the nose, for example. How deep is a "definite stop?"

My personal preference, and everyone has one, is a short, slightly upturned nose with a deep stop, the top of the nose level with bottom of the eyes. Some breeders feel this is too pretty a head; too "Pekey." Others want the nose level but by no means down.

The Standard specifies "one inch from tip of nose to stop." But more important than "one inch" is the overall balance of the head. All parts of the head must go together to produce a pleasing effect, and the head itself must be in balance with the rest of the dog.

Length of body and legs are other dubious characteristics. How short are short legs? How much longer a body is "somewhat?" And if the body should be longer than high, why do exhibitors push the tail high over the back to make the dog appear square? Why are breeders tending toward short backs? Because they can win with them? With short backs will come the straighter shoulder which will inhibit gait.

Photo study of a beautiful head and expression.

"HINDQUARTERS: Legs short, well boned and muscular, are straight when viewed from the rear . . . look massive on account of wealth of hair." This bitch displays her well-groomed "fanny" and a tail curled gaily over her back without any help from her handler!

112

The gait will, of necessity, become stilted and the true movement of the Shih Tzu will be lost.

There is nothing in the Standard that says a Shih Tzu should have a neck. Perhaps it is implied in GENERAL APPEARANCE by the statement, "distinctly arrogant carriage." True, it would be hard for a Shih Tzu to look very arrogant with a head sitting on its shoulders. On the other hand I've seen a couple of mighty arrogant looking bull-frogs sitting at the edge of our pool! However, it is taken for granted that most dogs have necks, and this includes the Shih Tzu. But should the neck be long and slim? If not, why are handlers thinning the coat from ears to chest to make the necks appear slimmer?

And while we are at it, how light is a "slightly lighter eye?" If eyes are "large, dark and round," is a large, dark, round BLUE eye permissible?

Perhaps these are niggling points in an otherwise aptly descriptive Standard, and one that wisely, after all it said and done, throws the ball squarely into the lap of the interpreter, whether it be breeder or judge, by the statement, "However, type and breed characteristics are of the greatest importance."

In 1981, the American Shih Tzu Club formed a Standard Clarification Committee to try answering some of these questions also posed by breeders. But why a clarification? Isn't such a document contrary to the Standard and a waste of a few people's time? Why not go to work on the Standard itself and clarify the obscure portions in it. According to the American Kennel Club the Standard is the description of the ideal dog of each recognized breed, to serve as a word pattern by which dogs are judged at AKC shows, and to define type, the characteristic qualities that distinguish one breed from another. But in addition to the breed Standard, there is a larger, more comprehensive standard which embodies the essentials of canine type and the characteristics which distinguish dogs from other animals and from *homo sapiens*.

The Standard for the Genus Canis

In order to breed Shih Tzu or any other dog breed, or in order to judge any dog, we must understand the canine standard as well as the applicable breed standard.

It's an irrefutable fact that type is vitally important in any breed and that without it, a judge might have a ring full of mongrels. But it is equally important to understand the functional principles of a dog's structure, which remain the same, whether the dog is a Shih Tzu or an Irish Wolfhound. They all have the same number of bones and muscles, and the way these parts fit together remains the same for all

Heads of male Shih Tzu may be larger than those of females and more doggy in appearance. There could be no doubt about the masculinity of this fellow.

Nor could the heartwarming expression of this face be anything but that of a bitch.

he warmly expressive eyes of this typical female are large, dark, round and placed wide apart. The quare, short muzzle has a definite stop. The overall feeling is one of good balance.

his six-month old female also shows the dark, rge, round eyes set wide apart and the top of the se level with the bottom of the eyes.

Just nine months old when this photo was taken, this young lady's eyes already are typically warm and full of expression.

115

This dog carries the "white blaze on the forehead and a white tip to the tail" specified in the modern British Standard and "highly prized."

"The hair on top of the head may be tied up." The word *tie* implies a ribbon or string, as opposed to the traditional elastic band shown in this unposed head study.

breeds. When a dog is correctly built, its movement will be smooth, graceful and efficient.

And while soundness and structure are not the distinguishing features of a breed, they are essential to health and locomotion. Without four legs that can move, two eyes that see, two ears that hear, there would be no dog shows, no judges and no breeders of the genus Canis.

A dog's ability to move and gait correctly usually means that the dog is sound and in balance. And the Shih Tzu is no exception. The way it moves tells us what structure lies beneath that luxurious coat.

"Slightly rolling, smooth and flowing gait with strong rear action" conveys the message clearly that the Shih Tzu is well angulated in the rear, with hocks remaining parallel to each other in motion as well as when standing still. The Shih Tzu's shoulders must be sufficiently laid back to complement its rear angulation for most efficient locomotion.

The front legs should move forward in a straight line with elbows neither in nor out. As it picks up speed the legs converge, moving into the center of gravity toward a point under the keel.

A Shih Tzu is not an Irish Setter and should not be raced around the ring. It should be shown at a natural, smooth, flowing gait so one

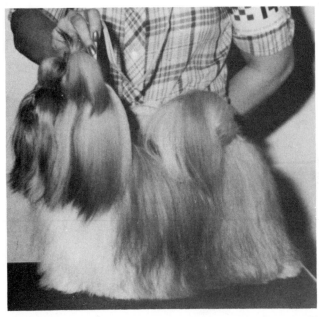

This lovely bitch perfectly illustrates the high set tail, which should be well-feathered and should balance the head set. The coat is luxurious as specified in the Standard.

The wealth of hair on legs and feet make them look massive. This lovely white and gold bitch, with black tippings graphically illustrates this point of the Standard.

Some Shih Tzu fanciers feel that a decorative bow, especially a check or polka dot, detracts from the balance and expression of the Shih Tzu; others feel it draws attention to the eye.

is able to detect the "slight roll." Neither should it be stilted in movement, with any noticeable rise or fall of the withers. It should move out, with a strong rear drive and a complimenting front extension. If well constructed, its short legs will carry it into a smooth flowing gait.

When a Toy is Not a Toy

Shih Tzu Standards from the earliest to the latest strongly convey the message that a Shih Tzu is NOT a Toy. The breed properly belongs in the Non-Sporting Group as it is classified in Canada, and every other country where it is shown with the exception of the United States.

Certainly, the Shih Tzu is a companion dog and has no purpose in life other than being gay and decorative. It doesn't hunt or go to

118

ground or catch mice. Although AKC classifies the Shih Tzu in the Toy Group, this is no excuse to disregard soundness, well-muscled legs, smooth, flowing gait and a sturdy body in favor of length and quality of coat. The beauty of a Shih Tzu is more than skin deep. It is a rugged, active, companion dog whose overall qualities should be appraised on the same basis as its cousins the Lhasa Apso or the Tibetan Terrier. It does not need to have any faults excused because it is a member of the Toy Group.

The Reverend Roger A. Williams provided a vivid description of Shih Tzu when he wrote:

> Look at the Shih Tzu outline as he stands proud, strong, alert, the embodiment of vigor.. . . see him move with his massive-looking fore-paws thrusting purposefully through the long dense hair of his coat, hindlegs flashing their pads as they drive the steady body, head carried high and tail forward, as free as a ship under full sail."

A BASKET OF JOY. Fortunate is the person who lucks onto one of these handsome puppies as a pet. The litter of six gold and white Shih Tzu, carefully bred by Clarence and Jayne Mann, is just five weeks old. It consists of two boys and four girls. A couple of them are destined for the show ring and the future of two more may rest in the whelping box, but the others will be sold as pets to loving homes.   *Brodbeck*

120

7

Buying, Training and Caring for a Shih Tzu Puppy

THE SHIH TZU makes a house dog *par excellence* and plays second to none. Centuries of breeding for just this purpose make it an excellent choice for anyone who wants a small, affectionate, handsome pet to care for and love.

How to Find the Right Puppy

Having decided that the Shih Tzu is the breed for you and that you have the time to take on the responsibility of a puppy and the grooming of a heavily-coated dog, don't be in a great rush to buy one. A puppy is not something to be bought on impulse. It will be a member of your family for many years. So take all the time you need to buy one that is sound in both mind and body.

Your first move is to write or phone the American Kennel Club, 51 Madison Avenue, New York, N.Y. 10010, an organization dedicated to protecting and furthering the interests of the purebred dog. It maintains an active file of hundreds of reliable, carefully selected breeders and breeding kennels all over the country. Upon request AKC will promptly send you the names of those in your vicinity that breed Shih Tzu.

Inquire also about any dog shows scheduled in your area in the near future. It is well worth the time to attend one or several and look carefully at the Shih Tzu in the ring. There are different types of Shih Tzu and many glorious combinations of colors and markings, and you may have or discover a personal preference for one or the other. You might even decide that this is a sport you would enjoy and would begin considering a show-quality puppy rather than a pet. However that's another whole bag of kibble!

After the judging is over, not before, talk to the exhibitors. Before judging they are busy concentrating on getting the dogs ready for the ring and don't like to take the time to talk to visitors. After judging they will usually return to the grooming area and will be happy to discuss the breed with you.

State your requirements as clearly as you can, if you know them. For instance, do you want a male or a female? Tell the breeder about yourself and be completely honest. How many children do you have and what are their ages? You live in a house, an apartment or a mobile home . . . you have a fenced in yard or prefer to walk your dog at necessary intervals . . . you have a large dog and want a small one and so on.

Even if you don't find the puppy you are looking for, you will come away with a new perspective of the Shih Tzu as a breed, and this awareness will add to the pleasure of having one of your own.

Make arrangements to visit the kennels of local breeders, but don't fall in love with the first puppy you see and don't allow anyone to pressure you into buying a particular specimen. A breeder who loves his dogs will never give you a fast sales talk. It is just as important that he finds the right home for his puppies as it is for you to find the puppy that is best suited to you both tempermentally and characteristically.

Some Thoughts on Price

Don't start out looking for a bargain, but try to obtain the best quality you can that is within your means. You may be willing to scrimp somewhere else along the line if you remember that your Shih Tzu will give you dividends in love and companionship for many years to come. The initial investment is comparatively small. And whatever the sum asked, you can be sure it is far less than the actual cost of the puppy to the dedicated breeder. You have to consider not only the time and money that have gone into raising a healthy litter, but the original sum invested in breeding stock and the cost of overhead to maintain them.

Puppies are individuals from day one. So listen carefully to any advice the breeder has. No one really knows the puppies as intimately as the breeder does. He has watched them develop mentally and physically from the moment they were born, and is certainly the one best able to evaluate the potential of any particular one in a litter. The one sleeping in the corner at the moment may just be the most mischievious of the bunch, and the aggressive puppy may be shy when taken from its "home base."

Although the objective in the heart of every reputable breeder is to produce only show-quality puppies, this never happens. In every litter there are one or more that fall short of the excellence required. They come from the same foundation stock, maybe from the same sire and dam but, because of some minor defect that prevents them from competition in the show ring, are sold at a fair pet price.

Price alone should not be the determining factor in your final selection. The majority of breeders are scrupulously honest and you will get exactly what you pay for. Remember, you are buying a purebred pet, not a show dog, so don't expect show quality at pet price. Remember too, that pets are just as healthy, strong and well-adjusted, raised in exactly the same way with the same amount of love and training as the ones with show potential. It is just that somewhere along the line, in the critical eyes of the objective breeder, a puppy fails to shape up for show.

Prices that established breeders ask for pet puppies are fairly well standardized in various areas throughout the country. Usually the closer to a metropolitan area the higher the cost.

Breeders do not accept credit cards and are seldom receptive to bargaining of any kind. Nor are they willing to let you buy a puppy on a monthly installment plan. Many, however, after an opportunity to assess you as a dog lover, something they can do with uncanny accuracy, may accept half-payment and the balance within a reasonable time. They will, of course, withhold ownership and registration papers until the puppy is paid for in full.

What the Buyer Should Know

While you are looking at the puppies, evaluate the kennel or dog room. Make sure it is clean and the dogs are well cared for.

Breeders should be willing to let you see not only the quarters in which the puppies are housed, but all puppies, whether for sale or not, and every dog that they maintain at the time. Be wary of the breeder

Two of the puppies, the boys in the background, are already in the show ring. The two girls in the foreground were sold as pets. Bred by Betty Nielsen, they were sired by Joy Tu's Shutterbug out of Chin Fo's Luv Po Shun. *Kennedy*

Litter brothers at three months of age. On left, Mei Shan Yankee Clipper was kept by his breeder for show, while Mei Shan Golden Sampan, right, was sold to a pet home. Both had the same sire and dam and were raised with the same amount of care. Breeder-owner is Patricia Burley. *Hoy*

who takes you into an anteroom and brings out one puppy for you to see. If the breeder is honest, he has nothing to hide and it is only by comparison that a buyer can judge the quality of a prospective pet.

Look at all the puppies the breeder is offering for sale. Watch them play. Do their eyes sparkle and are their coats clean and glossy? Their ears should be free of wax and inflammation. Their teeth should be white, their gums firm and pink. Their bones should be well-covered with flesh but there should be no pot bellies. Their muscles should be firm and they should be able to stand well up on their feet and move freely, ready to play with you or with their buddies.

Evaluate the breeder, too. You have every right to ask questions and, if you are knowledgeable in the questions you ask, it won't take long to distinguish between the true breeder and the one interested only in making a sale. Ask if he has the latest issue of *The Gazette*, the monthly magazine published by the American Kennel Club and the "bible" of the purebred dog fancy. Does he exhibit his dogs frequently at shows where competition is keen and points toward a championship are awarded? Are the sire and/or the dam champions? What about other champion ancestors?

Experienced exhibitors and breeders frequently use match shows, the kindergartens of the dog show world, as training grounds for puppies. Future hopefuls are exposed to the sounds, smells, and bustle of a typical dog show before they are six months old and eligible to be entered in championship competition. Seldom do serious breeders take wins at match shows seriously unless, of course, they win Best Puppy in Match. That's something to be proud of in any breeder's lexicon. But often buyers are impressed by breeders who display dozens of colorful ribbons as proof of the high quality of their dogs, without understanding the meaning of those ribbons. Read what is printed on them. If they were won at match shows or state fairs, where there is often little or no competition and where even a mediocre specimen can usually come home with a ribbon, they are little more meaningful than a bit of gay decor.

The breeder should be able to answer questions about the origin and history of the Shih Tzu and be informed regarding the breed's general care and personality. He should also be happy to give you a few tips on anything you should be particularly aware of concerning the puppy you may have chosen. He should have a veterinarian's certificate stating the puppy is healthy, free of external and internal parasites, and has had one or more protective inoculations. If further inoculations are required, the type of vaccine used and the due date should also be recorded on the certificate.

Barber's Mai Ling of Shang Tou, bred by Eleanor Eldredge, Seattle, Washington, was sold to Larry and Marci Barber when a healthy, happy well-adjusted four-month-old.

Responsibilities of the Breeder

The responsible breeder will urge you to have the puppy thoroughly examined by a qualified veterinarian of your choice within the first 48 hours after you take delivery. If anything is amiss, the breeder will be willing to take the puppy back and refund your money. This is as much protection for the breeder as for you, and the breeder will usually hold your check or cash from deposit until you have had the puppy checked out. Registration papers may be withheld until your check clears.

The breeder should show you how to groom your new Shih Tzu. If time permits, he will want you to watch your puppy being bathed and groomed, providing this has not been done before your visit to the kennel. You should also be given a complete diet chart, feeding instructions and a schedule covering the puppy's first year.

Often the breeder will give you a small packet of prepared food to take home with you so that any change in diet will not be too abrupt, and some will put together a "puppy care package," with a chewstick or marrow bone, a safe toy, and a handful of puppy biscuits or other such treat.

On Withholding Papers

Many breeders withhold registration papers on pet-quality puppies pending proof of neutering. Once the breeder receives a certificate of neutering (spaying or castration) from a qualified veterinarian, papers are transferred. This might be a verbal agreement between breeder and buyer but without a written, signed statement to this effect, the buyer can force the breeder to release the dog's papers. The verbal agreement will not stand up in court, if any money at all, even one dollar, exchanged hands, nor will the American Kennel Club take any steps to enforce it. AKC takes the stand that any such agreement must be the responsibility of the parties involved.

Without the backing of the American Kennel Club, and with proof of purchase, a breeder has no alternative but to sign over the papers.

The following quote from a letter from Pamela Mathews, Administrative Assistant at AKC, says it all:

> If a seller (breeder) feels that a dog, for one reason or another, should not be used for breeding purposes and if the dog is not neutered, the dog should be sold without papers. Our Rules do provide that a written agreement between buyer and seller, properly signed and executed to the effect that a dog is being sold with the understanding that NO AKC registration papers are to be furnished, will be honored.
>
> The recipient of such a dog could, under our Rules, apply for an Indefinite Listing Privilege which, if granted, would permit entry of the dog in

Obedience Trials and Tracking Tests only. The term *unregisterable dog* as used in connection with ILP applications includes a dog that is registered or eligible for registration with AKC, but that has been transferred with a written agreement between the new owner and the former owner, specifying that registration papers are not to be given.

An increasing number of dedicated breeders are accutely aware of the pet over-population problems and the hundreds of thousands of dogs euthanized each year at pounds and pet shelters throughout the country. For this reason they refuse to sell any pet-quality dog unless the buyer understands that no papers will be furnished. The breeder is anxious to protect the Shih Tzu breed from having any faults perpetuated, no matter how minor. At the same time he has invested a great deal of money, time and effort in building the quality and reputation of his kennel. It is only natural for him to want only the finest examples of his breeding used for propagation. And if you, the buyer, are honest with the breeder, you should not hesitate to sign such an agreement. "Pet" dog means that the animal, although purebred from the same litters as the breeding and showing prospects and equally sound and healthy, does not meet strict breed Standards and should NOT be used for breeding, adding more homeless pups to the present animal aggregate.

The following suggested agreement will hold up in the courts. It is generally printed on kennel stationery.

CONTRACT AND BILL OF SALE OF A PET SHIH TZU

Date: _____

Sold to: _____   _____
telephone number

_____

_____
zip

Name of Dog: _____ _____ Sex: _____
call name

Color: _____ Date of Birth: _____

Sire: _____ Dam: _____

Price: _____ AKC Registration Given? _____

Conditions of sale, if any:
Inoculation Certificate Given? _____Date of Recommended Booster? _____

Litter Registration No. _____ Ind. Registration No. _____

My purpose for purchasing this purebred dog is for companionship only. It is distinctly understood that it shall not be used for breeding by me or any other person. Should I sell or otherwise dispose of the dog, it shall be a condition of such sale that the new purchaser shall execute an identical agreement as this one and shall forward a copy of same to the American Kennel Club.

NOTE: This agreement may be cancelled by the mutual consent in writing of the parties hereto and for the payment of the additional sum of money agreed to: $_____ on or before: _____
                                                              date

_____   _____
Witness   Signature of Buyer

PET GUARANTEE: "Pet" means this animal is sold as a pet only and is not considered as breeding or showing quality per breed Standard. The seller guarantees that the dog is healthy and suggests examination by a veterinarian at the buyer's expense for the satisfaction of the buyer. If the veterinarian finds it diseased or crippled, purchase price will be returned upon the return of the puppy within 48 hours after purchase.

                                   _____
                                   Signature of Seller

ALTERATION AGREEMENT

I, the buyer, agree to have this dog neutered on or before the date agreed upon. AKC papers will be withheld until seller receives a statement verifying alteration completed by a certified veterinarian.

_____   _____
Witness   Signature of Buyer

The biggest problem with such an agreement is that it does not deter the unscrupulous buyer, who does not care if he has registration papers or not. Such questionable dog buyers only want breedable bitches to fill the demand for pets. In some mystical fashion, shady dealers can usually come up with "papers" if pressed.

Or it may be that the buyer already has a pair of registered dogs of questionable merit. It is very easy for him to register pups from his newly acquired dog or bitch in their name. It is even possible that he could hit the jackpot and come up with a winner!

Then there is the person who breeds his unregistered dog or bitch, purely through ignorance, not realizing that what he is doing is gross deception, tantamount to stealing. He is stealing the genes and chromosomes that the conscientious breeder is trying so hard to protect or perpetuating a serious breed fault, and for every pup he produces, he is eliminating a home for one of those soulful-eyed dogs "waiting their turn'' at the pound. There are just so many pet homes for dogs, and the saturation point has already been reached.

The Canadian Kennel Club stands behind a Non-Breeding agreement which has much in its favor. It permits registration papers to be given to the buyer of a purebred, pet quality dog, with the distinct understanding it is not to be used for breeding. Any progeny of the dog is not eligible for registration with the CKC, and the breeder is entitled to damages.

It is not infrequent that a puppy sold as a pet develops into a fine show prospect. Less frequently a monorchid (one testicle) drops the second testicle a few weeks after being placed in a new environment. In such instances, the cancellation clause and the fact that the dog has not been neutered, may be beneficial to both buyer and breeder.

It might behoove breeders in the United States to urge the American Kennel Club to adopt a similar procedure.

It is possible that the Canadian Non-Breeding Agreement might hold up in court in the United States. As far as I know it has never been put to the test.

THE CANADIAN KENNEL CLUB

Non-Breeding Agreement

I, _____
Name in full of buyer (PRINT IN BLOCK LETTERS)

of _____
Address

HEREBY CERTIFY AND AGREE THAT ON _____
Date

I PURCHASED OR OTHERWISE ACQUIRED A DOG FROM

_____
Name in full of person selling or otherwise disposing of dog

(HEREINAFTER REFERRED TO AS THE ''SELLER'')
ON THE DISTINCT UNDERSTANDING THAT

(1) Upon completing payment for the dog I am to be provided with a certificate of registration issued by THE CANADIAN KENNEL CLUB showing myself as the recorded owner of the dog.

(2) The dog shall not be used for breeding purposes by me or any other person and I hereby undertake to act as insurer in this respect and to pay the seller the sum of $ as liquidated damages for each time the dog is used for breeding purposes.

130

(3) Notwithstanding the payment of the aforementioned liquidated damages, any progeny of the dog shall not be eligible for registration in the records of THE CANADIAN KENNEL CLUB, nor may such progeny be represented as purebred.

(4) Should I sell or otherwise dispose of the dog, it shall be a condition of such sale that the new purchaser shall execute an identical agreement as this one and I shall forthwith file a copy of the same with THE CANADIAN KENNEL CLUB.

_____	_____
Signature of Witness	Signature of Buyer
_____	_____
Date	Address

Breed _____ Sex _____

_____

Name of Dog (if registered)   Reg. No.

Born _____, 19____ Color & Markings _____

Sire _____ Reg. No. _____

Dam _____ Reg. No. _____

I, _____
    Full name of seller (PRINT IN BLOCK LETTERS)

of _____
                    Address

HEREBY CERTIFY THAT THE ABOVE MENTIONED DOG WAS SOLD, OR OTHERWISE DISPOSED OF UNDER THE CONDITIONS STATED IN THIS AGREEMENT.

_____	_____
Signature of witness	Signature of seller
_____	_____
Date	Address

NOTE

(1) This agreement must be completed in TRIPLICATE. One copy is to be retained by the seller, one is to be given to the buyer, and the other is to be forwarded with the application for registration (or certificate of registration if dog already registered) and application for transfer of ownership to the Registration Division, The Canadian Kennel Club, _____
                                                                      Address

(2) This agreement may only be cancelled by the mutual consent of the parties hereto. Such consent must be on the "Consent to Cancellation" form (Canadian Kennel Club form #301). Any progeny born prior to the date

of the cancellation of the non-breeding agreement shall not be eligible for registration in the records of The Canadian Kennel Club. The Consent to Cancellation form, together with the certificate of registration issued for the dog, and the cancellation fee of $10.00, must be forwarded to: Registration Division, The Canadian Kennel Club, _____

Address

When you receive an individual registration application or certificate with the name of your dog on it, it must be returned to the American Kennel Club, with the required fee, if you wish to have the puppy transferred to your name. Anytime a purebred puppy changes hands, that change must also be registered with the American Kennel Club.

Male or Female

Small, regal dogs like the Shih Tzu, were bred to be beautiful house dogs. There is very little difference in the behavior patterns of the sexes. You'll find this especially true if you buy your pet from an experienced breeder who has raised it properly, lovingly handling it from birth. Perhaps the females are a little sweeter and the males are more dynamic and fun-loving, but males are not aggressive or oversexed and can be just as affectionate as females. The females, conversely, are just as smart and intelligent as the males. More depends on the temperament of the individual rather than its sex.

Like all other bitches, Shih Tzu will come into season approximately twice a year, but have little odor as they progress through their estrus cycle, and rarely if ever attract strange dogs to the house. Their color discharge is minimal and a negligible threat to upholstery or clothes. There are exceptions however to every rule. But, in general, the Shih Tzu's heats are no substantial problem. She must, of course, be confined to the house or to one room, should you happen to have a male dog as well as the female, and must never be allowed to run free. But the last rule applies whether she is in season or not.

Both sexes can be sexually neutered without altering their dispositions or personalities providing they are allowed to become physically and sexually mature prior to being altered. The operation is less expensive and considerably less complicated in the male than in the female. Any life endangering probabilities with either sex are due to the trauma of the operation, and to breathing difficulties of the short-nosed breeds such as Shih Tzu, Pekingese and Pugs. Breathing tubes have lessened the risk factor remarkably.

Both males and females housetrain easily. Certain situations may make a male forget temporarily, such as when a strange dog, especially a female pays a call, and bitches may forget their house training when

132

Almost all champions have at least one champion parent. Both parents of this sensational show puppy were Best in Show winners. Ch. Jazmin's Maxi-Million, bred and owned by Jackie Peterson is pictured finishing his championship at one year of age with his fourth consecutive major. This was BW at the Shih Tzu Fanciers of Southern California Specialty on June 30, 1979 under Wilma Hunter. "Max" was the only puppy in the litter and Jackie refers to him as her million dollar baby! By Ch. Dragonwyck The Great Gatsby out of Ch. Erincroft Qu Ti Pi of Jasmine, he was handled by William Cunningham.   *Rubin*

CANADIAN SUPER PUPPY. Can. Ch. Carrimount Au-So-Mr. Chan (Am. Can. Ch. Golden Frolic of Elfan ex Can. Ch. Carrimount Au-ChuChu), handled by Garrett Lambert, wins Best Puppy in Group at Canadian National Sportsmen's show in 1977 under Anna Katherine Nicholas. Just ten months of age, he was bred by Jeffrey Carrique and is owned by Mary Frothingham.

133

in season or during pregnancy. A little soda water rubbed on the soiled spot and a short refresher course usually solves any remissions from cleanliness.

Males, especially those not properly socialized, may cause minor embarrassment occasionally by attempting to ride a person's leg. This is seldom true of a Shih Tzu that has been adequately socialized in early months. Should your Shih Tzu try this, do not scold him. The best way to cure him is to distract him by playing with him or taking him for a strenuous walk.

Castrating a male, seems to strike terror into the hearts of many owners, especially men. Yet this simple, relatively painless operation makes calmer, more contented pets not only of Shih Tzu, which are fairly calm anyhow, but of all breeds of dogs and, of course, cats.

Neither male nor female Shih Tzu are coat shedders but, like your own hair, a few hairs are lost each day to be replaced with new ones. Females may lose quite a lot of coat when they come into season and again, nine weeks later when puppies would have been due had they been bred. Spaying your bitch corrects this loss of hair and is a wise precaution for the prevention of mammary tumors and uterine infection, which frequently develop in females as they grow older, whether they have been bred or not.

You may have firmly convinced yourself that nothing but a female or a male will do. But unless you have a very specific reason for the conviction, you would be wise to select the one that appeals to you the most at the time, without letting sex discrimination interfere with your decision. You may have to pay a slightly higher price for a pet male than a pet female, because the breeder knows that spaying a bitch is costly. But generally the price set by the breeder is determined by quality rather than by sex.

The Best Time to Buy a Shih Tzu Puppy

Buy your puppy when you are free to give it your undivided attention for at least the first few days; a long week-end, perhaps, or the end of a school year or before the beginning of your yearly vacation.

For those living in northern areas, Spring may just be the most suitable season because you will be able to take it out on nice days and introduce it to the great outdoors without fear of it catching cold. If you plan to exercise it routinely, you will be able to let it out at regular intervals or, if living in a city, can begin its curb training at a younger age than if you were knee deep in slush or snow. Shih Tzu love snow incidentally, and will play and romp through it like tiny long-haired snow plows. Always dry your dog or shake the snow out of its

Lying flat on tummy with legs stretched behind is a characteristically typical relaxed pose of the Shih Tzu. At 2 ½ months of age, "Cuddles" bred by Betty Nielsen, shows promise as a show dog.

By seven months of age, the show potential of a puppy should be obvious. This adorable puppy, Yen Von's Precious Penny (female), bred by Carol Rexrost and owned by Yvonne Carey gives every indication of growing into a show girl.

Ch. Jolei the Jazz Man owned and handled by Diane Kijowski. He finished with back to back majors at 18 months. He is by Ch. Jolei the Artful Dodger out of Chateau's Jolei Jasmin.

There have been many outstanding amateur owner-handlers. Diane Kijowski is one of these and Ch. Jolei Annie Oak-Lei is just one of the many Shih Tzu that Diane has finished. "Annie" was sired by Ch. Paisley Ping Pong out of Ch. Chateau's White Peony of Arlys.

coat and be sure to check between the pads of its feet for impacted ice.

Christmas Day is not a good time to bring a puppy into the home, unless you are prepared to protect it from the hustle, bustle and confusion of holiday activities. A puppy is much like a baby and needs its rest periods and plenty of love and reassurance that it is loved. A week before or, better still, a week after gives everyone time to adjust.

The Best Age to Buy a Pet Shih Tzu

Certainly NOT before a puppy is ten weeks of age can you or the breeder know what the individual will be physically or mentally. The smallest puppy in the litter may develop into the largest adult; the quietest may turn out to be hyperkinetic and supercharged with energy, and that strikingly marked flashy black and white puppy may just change, cameleon-like, into a vibrant gold and white.

The ideal time to buy a pet Shih Tzu puppy is when it is three to four months old. In contrast to dog sellers who unload their living wares as young as possible, before the cost of food and inoculations overtakes their profit, or before signs of unsoundness become dramatically clear, the reputable breeder will not chance selling a young show prospect as a pet. He might let go that "really great one" he has been working and hoping for for years.

By three months the breeder has a pretty fair idea of which puppies display show potential and which evidence minor faults in structure, movement or personality. Faults that would in no way inhibit a Shih Tzu's charm as a companion, but would rule out a show career place dogs in the well-bred pet category. Chances are you would never be aware of a particular fault unless the breeder pointed it out to you, as most breeders will. They are not trying to hide anything from you. Their sole reward is knowing they placed the right puppy in the right hands.

At three months of age the puppies are reduced to three meals a day instead of four, have had their last and most important permanent inoculation, and are stronger, less apt to be injured by a fall or careless handling, less apt to be stepped on.

By this time the puppies have been certified clear of internal and external parasites, are generally accustomed to the lead and to their bath and daily grooming. Their adult size can be fairly well calculated and their personalities have begun to unfold. The memory area of their brain is developed to the point where house-training can be accomplished very quickly. Your pet Shih Tzu will be in fine physical condition and psychologically it will be advanced to a point where you can be sure of a well-adjusted, outgoing, intelligent puppy, anxious to find its own home and have its very own people.

From three to four months is a critical period in a puppy's life. It is the stage of literally and figuratively cutting its teeth; a time for each puppy to develop its independence and self-confidence and to form a strong association with man. In its new home it will quickly develop its feeling of self-importance and become an individual.

It is up to you to discipline and train your puppy and to spend the necessary time caring for a three-month-oldster firmly, intelligently and, of course, with love.

Will an Older Shih Tzu or Young Adult Adjust to a New Home?

Anyone who has ever taken an older dog into his home knows how appreciative and devoted that dog is to its new family. The adjustment period may be longer than for a puppy but, once the older dog transfers its affection to you, it is more intense and just as enduring as that of any puppy.

Breeders of show stock are always hopeful that one or more in each litter will be outstanding show specimens. The first sorting of pet and show-potential puppies is usually made from three to four months, and those showing promise are kept by the breeder until they are at least six months or older. Occasionally one of these hopefuls will decide it does not like the noise, confusion and smells of a dog show and refuses to show with animation or to walk with its head well up. To be a show dog the Shih Tzu must live up to each and every sentence of the breed Standard, including the arrogant carriage specified under *General Appearance*, and without this show spirit in the ring, its chances of becoming a champion are slim. It may be the most beautiful example of its breed, exceptionally well-adjusted and loving but, without that special quality that sets it apart from its rivals, it cannot win honestly at shows where championship points may be awarded. These dogs are often offered for sale as young adults at reasonable prices.

In addition to these hopelessly recalcitrant young adults, a breeder is always on the lookout for people who would like to have a Shih Tzu for companionship but cannot afford the price of a puppy. Breeders, whose stock multiplies at a startling rate, will not put older dogs to sleep once their usefulness as producers is over. There are a few heartless, commercial breeders who euthanize their surplus stock, but the majority love their animals and are generally willing to let you have an older dog, perhaps a youngish bitch who cannot free-whelp, or a champion male the breeder no longer needs to sire future litters, for little more than the cost of having them neutered. They are equally agree-

This puppy superstar, bred by Arlys Kijowski and owned by Brenda McKnight, was just 8 ½ months old when he won a 3-point major at Colorado KC show. He is Ch. Loubren's Trail Blazer, by Ch. Jolei the Sundance Kid ex Nanjo Cactus Flower of Jolei and was shown by Max Kerfoot.   *Cott*

Another super puppy owned by Brenda and Louis Mc-Knight, bred by Arlys Kijowski and shown by Max Kerfoot is Ch. Loubren Pippi Long Stockings. This talented baby was BB over champions at just 9 ½ months under Erica Thomsen. He went on to win third in the Toy Group and completed his championship in ten shows at one year old.
                              Cott

Lisel's Sunnyside Up, by Ch. Lisel's Moshe Dayan out of Lisel's Tan-Ge-Rine, bred by Lise M. Miller and owned by Evelyn Clay, was pointed at the age of seven months.
                             Gilbert

139

DREAM GIRL. Ch. Abacus' Hazel Nutt, owned by Ruth Spivy, was only eight and one-half months old when she completed her championship. Bred by J.D. Basil and R.C. Smith and handled by Pat Jones, "Hazel" was sired by Ch. Abacus Brutha Nutt out of Abacus Pinkee Ring.   *Petrulis*

This charmer, Can. Ch. Jancrest Luvncare, earned her championship in just three days at seven months. She was top Canadian Puppy in 1979. Bred by J. Beath, she is owned by Rosemarie Hoo and is pictured winning one of her six Best Puppy in Show wins under Canadian judge Fred Fraser.

able, insistent in fact, that the dog be returned to the kennel within a couple of weeks, if the union is not a completely happy one. The last thing in the world a breeder wants is to have one of his dogs go from "pillar to post." Registration papers are not given in such cases but, once the adoption becomes a love match, the breeder will usually give you a certified pedigree. He is just as proud of your dog's lineage as you will be.

Either a young adult or an older dog can, most certainly form a close family association if given the opportunity by one who is patient, understanding and has a desire to make it work. If you are not this kind of person, you had better keep popping those quarters into the piggy bank until you have enough to buy a puppy.

Buying a Shih Tzu to Show

There are several ways to buy a show dog, but only one is fool-proof, and that is to buy an adult dog, already winning at championship shows, and immediately put it into the hands of a professional handler or agent.

This is the sure way, but also the expensive way, and the price commanded for the dog is commensurate with its wins and popularity at shows. Occasionally, one hears of $10,000 changing hands for a top show dog, and sums paid for lesser ones from $2,500 to $5,000 are quite common. In addition, there is the accumulating cost of the handler.

But this isn't at all what you have in mind. You want to do it yourself. It hadn't occurred to you to plunge into the big time. You just want to dabble your feet a bit in the dog show pool. But you want to win, of course—ribbons, lots of them; purple ribbons that mean championship points, and trophies galore!

What you don't realize is that this may be the expensive way in the long run, but guaranteed to be a lot more fun!

Your second best way to buy a Shih Tzu show dog, is to look for a puppy over six months of age. And your best place to do this is right at a dog show, fresh out of the ring. It should be lead trained and not timid or shy, a good representative of the Standard. It should move with good rear drive and an arrogant carriage. A shy puppy at this age will seldom outgrow this handicap. It should be aggressive, playful, look and act important. It should be in perfect physical condition for its age and should have had some experience, preferably having won at least one blue or first place ribbon in the puppy class at a championship show against competition.

Don't expect to buy such a young paragon of virtue for pet price. You'll be lucky if you can buy one at all, for any amount of money. Breeders are not anxious to sell their best puppies, that represent the culmination of years of careful breeding. They'd much rather keep them themselves and they are especially reluctant to let one go into amateur hands. They know that without proper exercise, care, grooming and training, the most promising show puppy can be hopelessly ruined. The breeder has already put more time into caring for and training the puppy than you could possibly pay for in dollars. What he wants is another champion to add to his list of homebred champions. What do you really have to offer? What can you guarantee?

It's up to you to court the breeder. Don't come on too strong. Take it easy. Get to know the breeder and give him a chance to get to know you. Your job is to convince him you are sincere and he will never regret a decision to sell you that dog. You may have to agree to a co-ownership with the breeder, at least until the dog becomes a champion, or guarantee to pay for the services of an agent of the breeder's choice, until you have had some show ring training yourself. And in addition to money, you may have to agree to a stud service on a dog or pick of one or two litters from a bitch. Don't get too involved with puppies back unless the breeder is of impeccable integrity.

There is still another method: That is to buy a promising three or four month old puppy from a reliable breeder who has bred many champions from championship lines, and to start praying. No matter how experienced, sincere and honest the breeder is; no matter how many champions he has bred or the number of champions in the puppy's pedigree, no matter how expert you become in handling the puppy, no one can forecast the outcome of a puppy at this age. And don't be taken in by someone who insists he can. It's hog wash! A puppy is a real gamble.

Study its pedigree. Is the dog inbred, linebred, an outcross of two linebred parents or a complete outcross? The closer related the parents are, the more your chances of knowing what to expect. Are its parents champions? Have they produced enough champions to have earned a registry of merit (R.O.M.)? One important statistic you should know: 75% of all champions have at least one champion parent.

From the time a puppy reaches three to six months of age many a major fault can surface. Mouths can go wry, the smallest puppy may stop growing, remaining too small to show; too small to breed. Kneecaps can slip, toplines can sag, males can pull up a testicle and retain it. But should you be lucky and none of these disasters befall your puppy; if it develops structurally and mentally the way the breeder hoped it would—then, maybe, you've got yourself a show dog.

Alaska's first Shih Tzu champion was Ch. Loretlargent Honey Bear, a 12-pound, gold with black mask, bred by Sharon St. Arnold. "Chad" is proudly owned by Virginia Coughlan and was handled to his championship by her daughter Barbara.

Ch. Lainee Hallucination, bred and owned by Elaine Meltzer, was Winners Bitch at the ASTC Specialty in Houston in 1979, making her a fourth generation Specialty show point winner. She is by Ch. Lainee Sigmund Floyd, R.O.M. out of Ch. Lainee X-tra Daffy.

143

Ch. Bel Air Diamond Jim (Ch. Jocliff Gentleman Jim ex Am/Can Ch. Bel Air Tif-A-Nee of Bamboo) was bred by Cathie Phillips and Diane Backovich and is owned by Elizabeth Chadwell. *Lindemaier*

Ch. Chaltenham Cricket of Nanjo, bred by Joan Cowie, finished very quickly owner-handled. One of her most exciting wins for owner, Richard Cullen, was her Toy Group second at Western Pennsylvania KA show in 1980. "Cricket" is closely bred to Ch. Char-Nick's I Gotcha and Ch. Afshi's Gunther.

144

Much Depends on You

Between three and six months of age a puppy's spirit and character are built. Both are important features of any show dog. And unless you know what you are doing, how to train your puppy, pose and gait it and show off its best features, it may never win a purple ribbon. Unless you learn to communicate with your dog at the end of the lead, you could be in trouble.

Handling a dog in the show ring is not as easy as it appears. Expert handlers are born, not made. However with determination, an inquisitive mind, an observing eye, with practice, many new exhibitors can become almost as good as the pros. On the other hand, if you spoil your puppy or fail in your responsibilities to it, you have nobody to blame but yourself. Don't blame the breeder. He has lost a great deal more than you have. He has lost another homebred champion.

If you don't fail your responsibilities to your puppy, and it develops a fault that makes it inadvisable to show it in the conformation ring, all is not lost. You can still give it the same training you would have if it had developed into a show dog and gain invaluable experience both at show handling and grooming. You can learn obedience with your dog and have fun earning a Companion Dog title with it. You can become "show-wise" and "ring-wise" and these abilities will stand you in good stead when the time comes that you find that "perfect" puppy, the one you couldn't pry loose from the breeder when you were a novice. And let's face it. When one Shih Tzu is good, two are better!

Keep in Touch with the Breeder

The breeder is your security blanket. Learn all you can from him. Listen to the advice, invaluable to you and your dog, that only its breeder knows. Eventually you will be able to sprout your own wings and find your own identity in the breed but, in the beginning at least, modesty is your most valuable asset. Respect and benefit from your breeder's years of experience. It's a foolish person who does not take advantage of what is freely offered for one's own good.

You're never going to buy a Shih Tzu puppy from me, because I've had my last Shih Tzu litter but, I'm going to offer you some free advice anyhow. After 25 years of continually learning and growing in the dog fancy, and I'm still learning and growing, the best tip I can give a newcomer is: Keep your eyes and ears open constantly and use your mouth only to ask questions.

BEAUTIFUL AND SMART, TOO. Ch. Imua The Gatsby's Pride of Ali-Aj, C.D. completed his championship as a youngster in just 12 shows. Two years later he began obedience training, earning his C.D. title in three shows with very high scores. Both his sire and dam were champions, so he came by his beauty and brains naturally. His sire was BIS Am. Can. Ch. Dragonwyck The Great Gatsby, R.O.M. and his dam was Ch. Imua's Wicked Wahine. He was bred by G. Sheduer but is owned and shown by Terri Castellano.

Ch. Chumulari Ying Ying

Ch. Dragonwyck The Great Gatsby

Ch. Mariljac Lotus Blossom

Ch. IMUA THE GATSBY'S PRIDE OF ALI AJ, C.D.

Ch. Lotos Panda Bear of Nanjo

Ch. Imua's Wicked Wahine

Ch. Nanjo's Haiku Dragon Brat

A handsome daughter of "Pride" is Ch. Ali-Aj New York City Splendor. She earned her championship points at 14 months of age in just three months of showing. "Splendor" was bred and is shown by owner, Terri Castellano. Her dam was Li-Ming Ms Smarte Pants of Ali-Aj.

How to Buy a Shih Tzu Show Puppy Without Any Money

Work for it! The majority of kennels are constantly looking for reliable and dependable help. There are always kennel chores and grooming to be done around Shih Tzu. At the same time you can learn about Shih Tzu, their general care and training and gain invaluable experience. You can earn enough money to pay for that show puppy when it comes along.

Lovely head study of Ch. Lainee Sigmond Floyd R.O.M. as a puppy, and, below, as a young adult, groomed for show. His moustaches and side head fall, and top-knot are tied with rubber bands to keep the hair out of mouth and eyes. Sired by Ch. Parquin's Pretty Boy Floyd out of Ch. Lainee X-tra Amorous, he was bred by Elaine Meltzer and Pat Gresham, and is owned by Elaine. He was top producing sire in both 1980 and 1981.

8

Bathing and Grooming Your Shih Tzu

THE ADULT SHIH TZU is an exceptionally hand-
some dog with a long, luxurious, dense coat. The hair on top of its
head is tied into a topknot to keep it from falling in its eyes, and the
topknot often sports a gay bow or barrette.

The Shih Tzu is a double-coated dog, meaning it has a long,
sometimes slightly wavy, outer coat and a wooly undercoat. And because of this double coat, it can be quite difficult to keep in good
condition. The wooly under coat may seem to mat overnight. It seems
to reach out and grab the top coat, which is more like human hair, and
wrap around it. If a mat develops it will be difficult to remove without
breaking some of the outer guard hairs, and the ends of the coat will
become broken and brittle.

Daily brushing keeps the skin clean and removes dead hair before
it has a chance to mat. It also stimulates the growth of new hair.

A Clean Coat is a Healthy Coat

Whether you bought your Shih Tzu for pet or for show, you will
want to keep it in top condition.

Your first grooming session should begin soon after you get your

There is a great selection of shampoos, conditioners and grooming equipment available to the dog owner. The indispensable pin brush is in the foreground on left, and a variety of steel combs is at right. In center are a toe nail cutter, forceps for removing hair from inside ears and cotton-tipped swabs for cleaning ear wax.

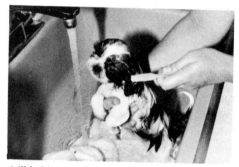

Still holding puppy securely, brush and clean hair on ears. Rinse thoroughly, being especially careful not to get water in its nose.

A small bath towel placed in bottom of sink prevents water from accumulating and gives a puppy secure footing. Holding the puppy securely under its chest with one hand, soak its body with lukewarm, running water, shampoo the body and rinse well. Leave the head until last.

A few minutes of cuddling in a towel reassures the puppy and soaks up excess water.

Carefully wet head with a wet sponge and clean the hair with "no tears" baby shampoo and a toothbrush, brushing the coat in the direction it falls.

puppy home, and it should be bathed once a week to remove the inevitable dirt which any long coated dog or puppy is bound to pick up from rugs, floor or grass.

Bathing and grooming procedures are basically the same for either a home companion or a show dog and your puppy has undoubtedly experienced both at least once or more often, depending on its age before it came to live with you. But now it is up to you to continue the bathing and grooming routines to keep your Shih Tzu clean and mat-free. A healthy coat is essential if you plan to show; it is your dog's crowning glory if you bought it just to love.

You should have a small grooming table or other sturdy table or counter with a non-skid surface. A comfortable chair at a convenient height, and a good light source round out furniture essentials.

You will need a good brush, a pure-bristle brush or, preferably, a pin brush with beveled pins. All pins should be straight and firmly placed in the rubber cushion. You will need a good quality stainless steel comb, again with beveled teeth.

Other equipment you will need for bathing and grooming your puppy are: A good quality protein shampoo, a bottle of "no tears" baby shampoo, a cream rinse or conditioner, a good pair of scissors, some latex elastic bands, a toothbrush, a multi-speed dryer and, sooner or later, you will have to have a good oil.

A Puppy's First Bath

During the first five weeks of life, your puppy had its face and fanny washed frequently with a face cloth and warm water, and at five weeks it experienced its first bath. It is important to introduce a puppy to its bath early in life, so it will associate it with a pleasant experience. Eventually it will learn to relax and enjoy the entire routine and the special attention given it at this particular time.

Grooming the Shih Tzu Puppy

Between bathing sessions, your puppy must be groomed every day or, at least, every other day, so you might just as well learn to do it right. Begin by brushing the coat on your puppy's tummy and chest. Sit in the chair by your grooming table, and spread a towel over your knees. Position the puppy on its back on the towel, tummy up, head toward your knees. Hold it firmly with one hand while talking to it reassuringly. With the other hand, brush the coat on chest and tummy with a pin brush or a pure bristle brush. Pay particular attention to the areas under the puppy's arms, legs and chin. In these areas mats are first apt to form. After brushing, run the large end of the steel comb through the coat. Be careful not to pull if you do find a mat. If a mat

151

develops, and it will, saturate it with cream rinse and, with the fingers start breaking and working it apart. When loosely matted, use the pin brush to gently brush out the remainder of the mat.

When tummy and chest have been brushed, fold the towel into a pad and place it on the grooming table. You are going to teach the puppy to lie quietly on its side during grooming operations. As your Shih Tzu matures, you will be spending more time at the grooming table and a dog that knows how to relax on its side while you brush its body coat will make it easier for you both.

Place puppy on the pad on its side, feet toward you. Continue holding it firmly while brushing the side of coat facing up. Turn puppy to the other side and repeat the brushing. Finally, set the puppy on all fours and part down center of its spine with the end of the comb or with a knitting needle.

It's unlikely, at this time in the puppy's young life, it will need to have the hair on top of its head tied. But, make believe anyhow to accustom it to what will come later. Brush hair on top of head back in the direction you want it to grow with one hand while you hold the puppy's head steady by gently grasping nose and muzzle with the other. Chin whiskers make a good handle and won't interfere with the dog's breathing. Sometimes it's not easy to grasp its short muzzle. As soon as the head hair grows long enough, accustom the puppy to having it held in place with an elastic band.

Getting More Serious

After a few brief test runs as described, your puppy will have become used to its introductory grooming routine. This is the time to discontinue dry brushing and learn to damp brush the coat, layer by layer.

Damp Brushing

Use a spray bottle with a fine nozzle that ejects a mist rather than a stream of water. Put a capful of light grooming oil or cream rinse, such as Alpha Keri bath oil, in the bottle and fill it with warm water. Dampening and layer brushing go hand in hand.

Layer Brushing

This is a grooming technique used on many long-coated breeds. It simply means that you are going to part the coat all over the puppy's body, beginning with the chest and tummy and proceeding to the sides, parting, misting, and brushing each layer until there is no possibility of a mat existing in the coat. If you leave one, the hair that you are

152

This puppy was born black and white, but will not stay that color. The lighter-colored hair next to the skin gives an indication of the color of the adult coat.

Use either a small hand dryer or a professional free-standing model. Low heat is normally all that is necessary. If the puppy shivers, it is usually due to nerves rather than from being cold. Avoid blowing the warm air directly into the puppy's face.

Nail clipping is best done with puppy positioned on its back on your knees.

A short play period mid way through the drying, helps distract puppy from noise and blowing air. The rubber mat on table assures a secure footing and gives the puppy confidence.

Puppy might just as well get used to lying on its back for later grooming of its chest and tummy coat when the coat grows long.

"Papa" checks to make sure all is well.

It's never too early to begin table training.

And when all is said and done, "I still love ya, Ma!'

154

cultivating will simply grow into the mat and the mat will become larger and more damaging. The layer technique guarantees that the entire coat has been thoroughly brushed, and the misting keeps it conditioned.

Correct Brushing Technique

There is a right and a wrong way to use the brush. The wrong way can damage the ends of the hair and is tiresome for the groomer. NEVER flick the brush. Use a rotary action with the wrist and, beginning close to the dog's skin, brush down to and beyond the ends. Learn to follow through with long sweeping strokes. With this method you will not lose hair and will be able to groom several dogs, if necessary, without tiring.

Bathing and Grooming the Growing Puppy or Adult Shih Tzu

Until about eight months to a year of age, the coat of a Shih Tzu is not difficult to care for if maintained in a regular, routine fashion. Show dogs should not be allowed to remain on carpets or on gravel or stone runs for any prolonged periods of time. The Shih Tzu loves to wipe its face on the carpet and static electricity breaks the coat and causes mats. Neither should show dogs be allowed to romp with other dogs, and when they come in from exercising, any debris accumulated in the coat should be removed immediately.

It is about this time that the adult coat begins to come in. It is usually coarser than the puppy coat. The puppy coat may drop out and, during this time, matting may be at its worst. This is when the owner of a show dog puts his dogs "in oil." The oiling of a Shih Tzu may mean anything from heavy cream rinse to olive oil. This will depend on the type of coat.

The purpose of oiling a dog is to keep the hair from matting, which causes breakage, but if the oil is not the right kind for the coat it may cause other problems. Your dog's breeder can direct you to what is right for your Shih Tzu's type of coat.

A light cream rinse is all that is needed for the Shih Tzu house pet.

A thorough brushing is a prerequisite to the bath.

When you are sure your dog is free of mats, place it in the sink on a terry cloth towel for secure footing. Slipping in the sink can damage the leg tendons and muscles.

Wet the dog thoroughly right to the skin with warm water using a spray attached to the faucet. Shampoo body first, before moving on to the head.

Detergent shampoos take the dirt out of white feet and legs and

Detergent shampoo takes out dirt on feet and legs, bleaches white hair and cuts the oil. Use detergents only on white areas and a regular shampoo for oily hair on colored areas, which will not lift the color. Two shampoos may be necessary to remove heavy oil, when getting ready for a show.

Use a toothbrush to clean whiskers, being careful to keep soap out of dog's eyes and water out of its nose.

Rinse soap out well with warm water and a strong spray.

Combine equal parts cream rinse and light oil, and pour through the coat. Put the stopper in the sink so the water may be used over and over through every strand of the coat.

Bundle the dog in a large, terrycloth towel to absorb surface water.

Place wet dog on its side on a dry towel and start brushing and drying tummy coat, working up side in layers to middle of side and up chest to its front legs, parting the hair at one inch intervals and brushing from the skin out. If the dog has not been freshly bathed, use warm water in a spray bottle and mist both sides of the parted coat.

Continue parting and brushing in layers up to center of back. Chest is done the same way, beginning at front legs and working up in layers to the chin.

157

Trim off hair between pads of feet.

Brush dog's legs next, starting with foot and brushing coat up toward hock. After feet and lower leg are dry, part and brush coat on upper leg in the direction of the toes.

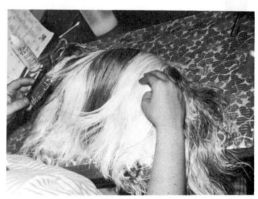

Turn dog to other side and repeat brushing and drying.

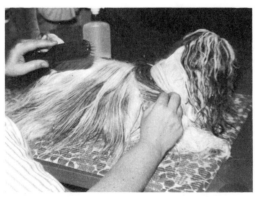

Place dog on tummy to brush and dry shoulders, working in layers gradually up the neck to the head.

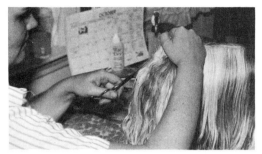

Trim off a small amount of hair around anus for cleanliness and part coat from back of neck to tail.

To keep long hair on top of head from breaking, part hair in center of forehead and secure each section over each ear with small latex bands.

Topknots should be brushed every day and latex bands changed. They disintegrate from the oil in the coat.

Comb should be used only on whiskers to dry face.

help bleach out any yellow in the white coat. At the same time, if the dog has been kept in oil between baths, it cuts the oil.

By the same token a detergent will also lighten colored coats and may be why some exhibitors feel it is necessary to "enhance" the color of their Shih Tzu. Detergents should not be used on gold, red or black coats, and only on the white areas of parti-colors. There are many good "people" shampoos, preferably with conditioners added, available at drug stores, supermarkets, and beauty supply outlets, that will cut oil.

If your long-coated dog has been kept in heavy oil, it should be bathed two days prior to a show. This preliminary bath releases the oil. Bathe again, with two thorough sudsings, prior to the show.

Sure it is more work, but worth it. You will maintain a healthy, shining coat as well as your integrity.

If Your Shih Tzu Becomes Matted

The best way to keep your Shih Tzu free of coat-destroying tangles and mats is to not let them develop in the first place. If you do, you and your dog will have to endure many hours of tortuous grooming to save its coat. Washing a matted dog only makes the condition worse. If the mats are so bad that they cannot be worked out with cream rinse, fingers and brush, you may wish to try soaking the dog in oil.

Dry the dog, slowly working out the mats. When it is totally free of mats, bathe it again in the normal way and reoil.

Trimming

Overtrimming is wrong, but a little makes a neater-appearing dog. Usually long, straggly looking hairs are trimmed from around the feet, and a little is taken near the set-on of tail. Do any trimming gradually. You can always cut more, but you can't put it back if you cut too short. Watch other breeders at shows to learn all you can about their grooming tricks and "secrets."

Face Washing

The hair on the face of the Shih Tzu, especially any that is white, is easily discolored. To help prevent discoloration, wash and comb the face daily. Use a "no-tears" baby shampoo.

Since it is only the face you want to wash, keep the dog's body coat dry by setting it into a heavy-duty plastic trash bag, large enough to let it sit comfortably. Fasten it around its neck with a hair clip or clothes pin.

Moustache and beard are particularly susceptible to staining from food or even from water. If stained, apply cornstarch to the stained

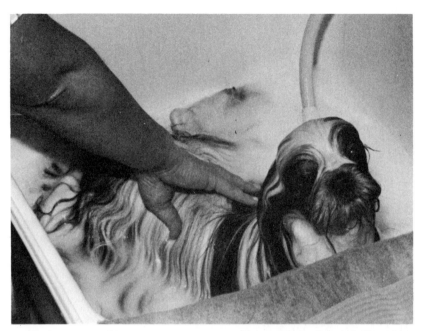

Put the dog on a towel in a sink half-full of the combination cream rinse and oil you have worked out for his coat. Let it soak in the solution for five minutes, ladling the solution over and through its coat. Some of the dirt will come out in the solution and may make the mats easier to pull apart.

Mother and daughter look neat and comfortable in their kennel trims, yet maintain characteristics of their breed.

Ch. Lisel's Tangerine has been freshly bathed, and her long topknot has been artistically trimmed away, leaving her long ear fringes.

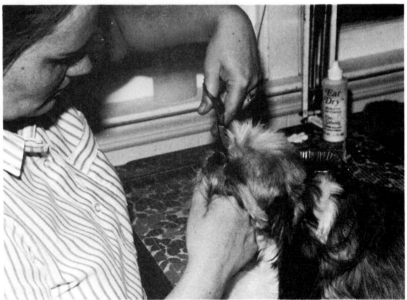

Trimming away the long hair from top of nose and between eyes, prevents tearing, and magnifies her large, soulful eyes and warm expression.

All how-to photographs in this section were taken by Alan Miller, and the grooming was done by the well-known breeder Lise M. Miller, without whose participation and cooperation, this book would have been much more difficult to complete.

162

After a dog is retired from the show ring, before a bitch is due to experience motherhood, or for ease of maintenance, there are several attractive trims that can relieve both you and your dog from tedious coat care.

One type of kennel trim, shaves all the coat from belly and cuts the back coat short, leaving a moderate amount of coat on sides and chest.

Hair on tips of feet is shaved and hair on bottom of pads and between the toes is removed. This keeps the feet dry and prevents them from collecting every leaf and stick in the garden.

In a more extreme trim, feet are shaved like a Poodle's, and all side coat is cut short.

163

area while hair is damp. Work it in with the fingertips, allow to dry, then comb or brush it out thoroughly, again being careful not to get any in either the eyes or the nose.

Ears

Ears on drop-eared breeds like the Shih Tzu need special attention. After a bath the ears should be cleaned with a cotton swab dipped in mineral oil or Panolog. To avoid accidental injury to the eardrums, fluff the cotton out from around the end of the swab with fingertips. Wipe the ear clean and dry with another swab, being careful not to dip too deeply into the ear, damaging the eardrum. Damp ear canals promote the growth of bacteria and fungi, which can cause infection. They are also a perfect environment in which ear mites can thrive. If ear mites are allowed to persist for any length of time, they can cause an inner ear infection, which can be fatal if it reaches the brain.

Ask your veterinarian for advice, should you suspect ear mites. He will give you medication to put into the ears for several days until the mites are destroyed.

Usually a brown discharge with a foul smell is your tip-off for mites, plus the dog constantly scratching and digging at its ears.

Eyes

A Shih Tzu's eyes are large and vulnerable and prone to ulceration. Special attention should be given to them daily. Living close to the ground, it is easy for dust or dirt or a stray hair to get into the eye and cause irritation.

Use human eye wash daily, such as Collyrium. This is a gentle eye wash. Fill an eye-dropper with the solution and flood the eye with it.

Remove any accumulated matter from eye corners with the fine end of a comb. A flea comb may be used on pet dogs to remove any dried particles of food that may be trapped in beard or moustache. Show dogs should have the particles brushed out with a toothbrush after a bath or after a face wash, when face furnishing are wet.

164

9

Your Shih Tzu in Sickness and in Health

$\mathbf{T}$HE SHIH TZU is an extraordinarily healthy dog but, like every other dog must be immunized against infectious diseases in puppyhood and from then on, at least once a year. It needs the right amount of high-quality food, plenty of fresh air, exercise and sunshine and thrives on more than a dog's share of love and affection.

Years of pampering in the palaces of the Orient have endowed the Shih Tzu with the need of a close association with people. It is in essence a "family" dog and belongs in the heart of the home as an integral member of the household. It does not thrive in the isolated, impersonal atmosphere of a large kennel.

Fortunately, Shih Tzu also enjoy the companionship of each other, making it possible to maintain several in the home as both companion dogs and show dogs, providing one has time to give them the necessary coat care to maintain show condition.

The big drawback in allowing the show Shih Tzu to be a house dog is that constant romping and rubbing against chair legs and sofas are not conducive to coat growth. The ends of the coat are being constantly broken and, while the dog will develop a thick undercoat, the long guard hairs will not reach any great length.

It becomes almost necessary for any exhibitor, anxious to win more than just championship points, or for the small breeder to have individual cages or pens where his dogs can be confined for rest periods, when you may be out of the house and not able to supervise activities, and to sleep for the night. They are also advantageous at feeding time. When dogs are fed separately, you know which ones ate well and which ones didn't. Occasionally a normally good eater will decline food and should be watched in case some illness is developing. The pens should be placed as close as possible to the main stream of activity in the home, preferably in a small room off the kitchen or family room. As the number of adult dogs grows, as it is apt to do, it may become essential to have separate areas for stud dogs and bitches in season, and a quiet draft-free room for whelping.

If Your Shih Tzu Becomes Ill

We all hope our dogs will never experience illness or injury but we should be prepared to recognize when a dog is sick or hurting and know how to cope with it.

It is not within the scope of this or any breed book to deal comprehensively with canine health problems and first aid treatments. The best we can hope to do is skim the surface and provide warning notes as to when it is imperative to seek veterinary help.

The American Veterinary Medical Association has published a list of signs, which are reasons for seeking a veterinarian's advice. None would be considered emergencies, but are symptoms which should be evaluated in relation to general good health.

1. Abnormal behavior, sudden viciousness or lethargy.
2. Abnormal discharge from nose, eyes or other body openings.
3. Abnormal lumps, limping or difficulty getting up or lying down.
4. Loss of appetite, marked weight losses or gains, excessive water consumption, difficult, abnormal or uncontrolled waste elimination.
5. Excessive head shaking, scratching and licking or biting any part of the body.
6. Dandruff, loss of hair, open sores, or a brittle dull coat.
7. Foul breath or excessive tartar deposits on teeth.

Before calling your veterinarian, take your dog's temperature with a rectal thermometer. Don't make guesses by feeling its nose. A dog's nose is no barometer of body temperature.

How to Take a Dog's Temperature

Shake down the mercury in the thermometer below 90 degrees. Lubricate the bulb end with Vaseline or KY jelly and insert it gently into the dog's rectum. Talk to it and rub its tummy for the two or three minute duration specified by the manufacturer of the thermometer for a correct temperature reading.

A dog's normal temperature can range from 101 to 102 degrees Fahrenheit. If above or below this normal range, consult your veterinarian. Many minor ailments may be safely treated at home, but don't resort to home remedies before checking with your veterinarian.

If your Shih Tzu is still a puppy, don't waste any time securing aid at the first indication of trouble. Quick and accurate diagnosis is important because puppies have less resistance to disease and illness than mature dogs, and some of the small breeds have little tolerance for stress of any kind.

Until you can get your puppy or dog to the veterinarian, keep it quiet and out of drafts. Stay near and let it know you love it. This is a time when your dog needs you most. He needs the comfort, love and reassurance that only you can give.

No medication or injection of any kind should be administered to your dog without veterinarian approval and, within every dog owner's home, there should be a copy of *The Dog Owner's Home Veterinary Handbook*, by Delbert G. Carlson, D.V.M. and James M. Griffin, M.D., published by Howell Book House. It is a comprehensive dog care guide for the layman and deals intelligently with emergencies, infectious diseases, burns, environmental exposure, hypothermia, heat stroke, poisonings, fractures, seizures, shock and much more. In simple terms it tells you what you can safely do to treat your dog and when to consult your veterinarian.

Kidney and Urogenital Diseases in the Shih Tzu

A kidney disease known as *renal dysplasia* is common in the Shih Tzu breed. It bears some similarity to kidney disease in the Lhasa Apso. Whether the disease is inherited is not yet known but a good deal of evidence points a suspicious finger in that direction.

The occurrence of renal disease in the young Shih Tzu puppy and the fact that usually more than one puppy in a litter and, in some instances, the entire litter is affected leads us to suspect it is inherited and that every effort should be made by Shih Tzu breeders to avoid breeding any stock whose former offspring have been affected. Currently the disease is irreversible and death is inevitable.

Extensive tests have been carried out by Dr. Bovee of the University of Pennsylvania in cooperation with the American Shih Tzu Club. The first of three reports prepared for Shih Tzu breeders was recently published in the *Shih Tzu Bulletin*, dealing with kidney disease in general. The others will define the specific disease found in Shih Tzu, and describe its genetic mode of inheritance.

The functions of the kidneys are complex. Their primary purpose is to regulate body fluid balance. They are essential to eliminate metabolic acids and other waste by-products of urea from the body, and without functioning kidneys, the dog cannot sustain life.

Kidney disease may have many causes which include infection, obstruction, ingested toxins or poisonous compounds or abnormal development. There are three stages of development. Unfortunately there are no clinical symptoms of early renal disease which may progress over a period of months or years to the second stage, when symptoms first become obvious. The affected dog will develop an excessive thirst and will pass greatly increased amounts of urine. The urine will appear to be very diluted or watery. Some dogs will be listless, poor eaters and may suffer a weight loss. In the final stage, the symptoms of stage two are more pronounced and may be accompanied by severe depression, diarrhea, vomiting, and dehydration all evidences of kidney dysfunction which will sooner or later result in coma and death. This acute kidney involvement is known as *nephritis*.

Diagnostic tests such as blood urea nitrogen, known as BUN, plasma creatinine and urinalysis can be performed by a qualified veterinarian to confirm the presence and severity of kidney disease. Each of these tests measures different components of kidney function. Low urine specific gravity may indicate the presence of renal disease but there are many unrelated diseases which can cause diluted urine and only your veterinarian can differentiate between them. Blood and urine collected for these tests should be taken after a 12 hour fast.

Renal disease runs high in all breeds of dogs. After the age of eight years, 85 percent of all dogs have some kidney degeneration or will have developed chronic nephritis. This is known to be a congenital, hereditary progressive kidney disease in certain breeds, whereby the kidneys do not maintain sufficient function to sustain life.

Kidney and Bladder Stones

Many smaller dog breeds are predisposed to kidney or bladder stones or those that collect in the duct connecting the kidneys to the bladder. These lower urinary tract diseases express themselves in an increased stimulation to urinate or the inability to do so. The male may strain and make frequent attempts to urinate with little result; the female may pass a few drops of urine, walk a few steps and pass a few drops more. If the dog is unable to urinate it becomes an emergency and, unless the obstruction is surgically removed, the dog will die of uremic poisoning.

168

Stones occur more frequently in males than in females because of the male anatomy. The urethra in the male is small and can easily become obstructed by a stone. The urethra in the female is larger and less prone to stone development.

Many such obstructions, however, have been successfully removed but will develop again unless the dog is kept on preventative medicine. And in order to prescribe the correct medicine the mineral composition of the stones must be analyzed. Phosphate stones are the most common and a greater incidence of this type is found in the female than in the male dog. They are associated with alkaline urine and frequently with a bladder infection.

Urate stones, composed of uric acid are more frequently found in the urinary system of males and in these cases the urine is acid.

Cystine uroliths, composed of the amino acid cystine, make about five percent of all stones and occur exclusively in males. It is an inherited defect, wherein cystine is reabsorbed into the kidneys rather than be excreted in the urine and it accumulates in the bladder where stones form. They must be removed by surgery.

A Bit of Flower Power, Am/Bda. C.D., finished his title by winning high-scoring Toy dog at the Bronx County Kennel Club show. The judge, William Hutchins, holds the ribbon, while Karolynne McAteer, his proud owner-handler, kneels by "Peanuts."

10

The Shih Tzu in Obedience

TODAY IT IS GRATIFYING to see more and more Shih Tzu being trained and shown in obedience competition. Intelligence is basic to every breed, and obedience is one of the best ways to prove that Shih Tzu are not "beautiful but dumb." Shih Tzu are not difficult to train. Some may have greater natural aptitude than others, just as in any other breed but, basically any Shih Tzu can be trained if the trainer uses knowledge and patience. It all depends on the human connection.

Most Shih Tzu want to please their owners, a helpful trait in the obedience ring and a characteristic bred into them. Throughout the Shih Tzu's entire history its primary purpose in life has been as man's companion. They were valued for their beauty and affectionate disposition. But no matter how adorable and even tempered, your Shih Tzu can be easier to live with and more pleasure to own if it is taught good manners.

It is not the purpose of this chapter to deal in depth with obedience training. There are many excellent books devoted to the subject and many training schools where you can learn to teach your dog basic obedience. The exercises and all the rules concerning them can be obtained by writing the American Kennel Club, 51 Madison Avenue, New York, N.Y. 10010 and asking for the booklet *Obedience Regulations*. You must thoroughly understand these rules if you plan to show in obedience and earn the scores necessary to add the various obedience titles after your dog's name.

Obedience training teaches YOU to control your dog and the obedience judge looks for a team that works well together.

Where obedience classes will be held and when they are due to start are usually advertised in local newspapers by area training clubs. You might be able to find out about them through people you know who have trained or shown dogs in obedience or see them posted in your veterinarian's office. Most begin a series of classes every two or three months.

Before signing up with any class in particular, visit several and question anything you don't understand. Bear in mind that correction is a necessary part of obedience. Correction is not punishment, and need not be abusive in any way. Correction and communication are inseparable in training your Shih Tzu. You show your dog what you expect it to do, then help it execute the exercise, correcting it gently but firmly when it goes wrong, and encourage it to do it your way.

Once your dog knows what you expect of it, you can begin to enforce your commands with a combination of consistency and praise. If you want a consistent performance out of your dog, you must be consistent yourself. So, find the instructor who is best suited to teach you an intelligent, humane training regimen, remembering always it is the instructor's job to train you rather than your dog.

How well or how quickly your dog learns an exercise depends totally on you, your attitude, the attention you give your instructor and the amount of time you give to the dog's training. It takes plenty of Patience, Praise and Practice—the 3 P's of obedience. The exercise must be repeated over and over again so your dog does not forget what it has learned. Usually trainers require more practice with small dogs than with the larger breeds. Dogs are just as individual as people and must be trained accordingly. Of the three P's, praise is by far the most important if you are going to have a happy, willing worker.

Entering your Shih Tzu in obedience training classes assures a well-mannered dog both at home and away. It does not necessarily mean you have the ambition to compete in obedience trials at American Kennel Club sanctioned events where obedience competition is offered. However, if you enjoy competitive sports, you might easily be tempted to try earning an AKC obedience title with your Shih Tzu.

Each exercise is designed for a reason and has a practical application in a dog's behavior at home. They apply equally to dogs of any size. After all, size does not constitute intelligence and high intelligence often comes in small packages.

Graduation

The last session in each training class series is graduation night. You and your dog will compete with the other members of the training class just as you would if you were entered in an obedience trial at a dog show.

Usually you will be given a certificate of graduation, meaning that you completed the required number of lessons, no matter if you make a low score or a high one. It does not give you any *leg* toward an obedience degree. *Legs* can be awarded only at authorized obedience trials.

Novice, Open, and Utility Obedience

In the fascinating and absorbing world of obedience training, you have just graduated from Kindergarten, known as Sub-Novice. If your dog did well and showed enthusiasm for its work you may want to continue lessons, advancing into Novice obedience. When you and your dog become proficient in Novice, you can both continue your education in Open obedience and finally the ultimate in obedience training—Utility.

The same basic six commands learned in Sub-Novice training apply to the most advanced and complicated exercises.

In Novice, you will repeat the exercises learned in Sub-Novice. The difference is you will be working without a leash, proving you have control over your dog.

In Open obedience you will continue the off-leash exercises, but will go on to more advanced training, teaching your dog to drop instantly on command. This proves your control over your dog even if it is just chasing a cat. You will teach it to retrieve a dumbbell on command, both across the room or ground and over a high jump, and to remain in both sitting and lying position while you are out of sight.

Utility obedience takes you and your dog into much more demanding areas, requiring both intelligence and willingness to work well. These exercises bring the dog's senses into play. It will be required to identify your scent from objects made of wood, metal, and leather. It must retrieve an article you pretend to have lost by a combination of scent detection and retrieving. It will learn to obey by hand signals alone, with no dependence on the spoken word. It proves your dog understands and is willing to obey commands to STAY and JUMP without being at your side. The last test of your dog's intelligence is learning to STAY, without moving out of position, to allow a stranger to examine it without exhibiting fear or resentment while you are some distance away.

AKC Sanctioned Obedience Trials

There are three distinct classes: Novice, Open, and Utility. Both Novice and Open are divided into two categories, A and B. The exercises in both are identical, but in A the dog must be handled by its owner or a member of the family, and only one dog may be entered, while in B, professional handlers, trainers, and others may enter, and an owner may enter more than one dog, providing it has a separate handler for the SIT and DOWN exercises, which require group participation.

Obedience Titles

A dog must earn passing scores in the Novice class at three shows to earn the title of Companion Dog. This entitles the owner to enter the initials, C.D. after its name.

A dog must earn its C.D. before it may be entered in Open. Once again it must win passing scores at three shows to earn the title of Companion Dog Excellent, or C.D.X. and must earn its C.D.X. before it can compete in Utility classes. Another three passing scores awards it the initials U.D. or Utility Dog, the highest title a dog can win in obedience trials at dog shows.

Toby Tyler and a Story of Persistence

Pat Di Nardo had always been interested in obedience as a spectator. She did not begin to train Toby until he was almost two years old. Toby was an only dog and totally spoiled, and Pat wasn't sure how he would respond to obedience training. Loving Toby very much, she would not have continued training him if he hadn't taken to it. Now whenever he sees Pat pick up his obedience lead, his tail begins to wag and he runs to the door to wait for her. If she takes too long getting there, he begins to bark!

Pat and Toby finished basic classes (ten weeks) at the end of August, 1979 and proceeded to attend advanced classes for C.D. work.

Training came along nicely for the next three months but, with December, the cold and the snow, their progress stood still through the winter.

In the spring, Pat began showing Toby in Sub-Novice at match shows. She continued through two more weekly training sessions and

BEAUTIFUL BUT NOT DUMB. A lovely head study of Collet's Toby Tyler, Am/Can. C.D. owned by Patricia Di Nardo in Pittsburg. He is out of Ch. Chumulari Chung Hsia Te, a daughter of Ch. Chumulari Ying Ying.

"Toby" in his "work clothes," with dumbbell in mouth. Shih Tzu are happy workers and easy to train for the obedience ring.

175

worked Toby every day either at home or at shopping centers. It took five match shows before Toby earned a qualifying ribbon.

During the winter of 1980, Pat and Toby gained the confidence they needed to enter a real show but, the first that was going to be held in her area was not until March, 1981, so Pat entered Toby in a February match held at a shopping mall on a busy Saturday. The ring was surrounded by curious spectators, and when Toby entered the ring there was lots of "ooing and aahing" from the shoppers. Toby was no dummy! When he and Pat began the off-lead heeling, Toby left her side and went over to the crowd to collect the attention personally. Needless to say, Toby did not qualify but, if the club had offered a personality award, Toby would have won it!

Finally the day of Toby's first real trial arrived. It was the large, important Western Pennsylvania KA show at the Civic Center in Pittsburgh. Forty dogs were entered in Novice A and Pat was understandably nervous. As she and Toby stood at ringside waiting to go in, the *Star-Spangled Banner* was played. Pat wrote, "the combination of everything made me feel as if this were the most important day in my life! I'll never forget my emotions as Toby and I waited. This was it!" She didn't want the day to ever end.

Both Pat's instructors were there to share the thrill of Toby's first leg.

Not believing for a second that Toby would win all the time, Pat had him entered in six shows. Toby earned his C.D. at the first three and continued to qualify in all six—in less than three months! Toby continued on to earn his Canadian C.D. also in three trials with scores of 194, 190 ½ and 187!

The Story of "Omar," the Utility Shih Tzu

Omar Play Boy, U.D. owned and shown by Mary Hollingsworth, was the first Shih Tzu to earn the title of Utility Dog. What dog and owner accomplished as a team in a very short time was incredible.

Mary entered Omar in obedience training classes mainly out of curiosity. Once they got started, it was a different story because they quickly developed interest, even though from that first day the odds were against them.

Omar was a very intelligent Shih Tzu but, like most of the breed, according to Mary, was quite stubborn and hard to work with at times.

During basic training, Mary admits that she and Omar were usually two or three weeks behind the progress of the rest of the class. Omar would run between Mary's legs when anyone came toward him during the STAND-STAY exercise. The STAND-STAY and the DOWN

Omar Play Boy, U.D., Canadian C.D. sits amid some of his ribbons and trophies.

The following action pictures were taken by Mary Hollingsworth.

Omar jumping bar jump in directed jumping exercise.

Omar jumping high jump in directed retrieve exercises.

Omar returning glove in directed jumping exercise.

Mary has always liked this picture because she doesn't think people realize how difficult it is for a small short-nosed breed to pick up and hold on to a glove.

Omar finding and returning metal article in scent discrimination exercise.

178

Omar returning leather article in scent discrimination exercise.

Mary Hollingsworth, Omar's trainer, exhibits not only in obedience, but in conformation. Here she waits at ringside with Shente's Mr. Mac Barker for the photographer to record the dog's first major.

Omar had to overcome his fear of large breeds. Here he practices the long sit-stay next to a towering Doberman.

179

were difficult exercises to conquer, but conquer they did, placing second out of 35 at their graduation.

After being disqualified at both their first match show and their first regular obedience trial, they earned the first two legs toward Omar's C.D. back-to-back at Ravenna and Chagrin Valley shows.

Another disqualifying score came in Indiana, where Omar skipped off to a corner of the ring to clown for the spectators, leaving Mary to heel by herself. But at the next show they not only won their third leg with a score of 197 ½, but a trophy for highest scoring dog in the Toy Group.

That was all Mary needed to continue work in Open. She joined the Columbus All-Breed Training Club in Columbus, Ohio, for which she is now an instructor. She set up jumps in her basement, where she and Omar worked for six full weeks before she could get him to take the dumbbell willingly in his mouth. When Omar finally made the breakthrough, his tail going a mile a minute, it was hard to know who was happier, Omar or Mary.

From there on everything was up and Omar became a C.D.X. before any of the rest of his class. With scores of 196, 197 and 196 ½, he earned the Award of Canine Distinction given by *Dog World Magazine*, and became the second Shih Tzu to earn a C.D.X. The first was Tohatsu of Sherilyn, owned and trained by Sherry Heldman.

By this time Mary coveted the title of Utility Dog and was determined to try to make Omar the first Shih Tzu to earn this difficult title. Few trainers believed that a Shih Tzu could get past the scent discrimination exercises, but Mary knew better and, as it turned out, that proved to be their easiest Utility exercise. Omar caught on right away and after six weeks of intensive training, they worked up to eight scent articles in four days!

One year later, in September, Mary entered their first show at the same place where Omar had clowned in the ring when working for their C.D. He qualified, only to fail in his next three shows. He earned his second leg at Dayton and a third at Cleveland on October 29th. Omar and Mary not only did it, they did all their utility training and showing in exactly three months. Omar became the first Shih Tzu to earn a Utility Degree, and at just two years of age.

Handsome is as Handsome Does

Helen's Brandy, U.D. is the third Shih Tzu ever to add the initials O.T. Ch. before his name, meaning obedience trial champion. Brandy, owned by Helen and Harold Cash and handled by Harold, obtained all three degrees, C.D., C.D.X., and U.D., in less than nine months and

O.T. Ch. Helen's Brandy. U.D.

In the directed high jump exercise for utility, a jump is placed on each side of the ring. One is the regular jump used in Open Exercises, and the other is a bar jump. The handler sends the dog about 50 feet away from him and commands it to sit. The dog must then clear whichever jump the handler directs. The exercise is repeated until each has been jumped. On the right Brandy takes the high jump in his stride. On the left, he happily clears the bar jump. Each jump is considered half the exercise.

181

Brandy "flies" over the broad jump, an open class exercise. The length of the jump is two times the height of the high jump. For Brandy this adds up to 28 inches.

Retrieve over the high jump is another open class exercise. Here Brandy retrieves a dumbbell over the high jump, which is one and one-half times the height of the dog at withers. Brandy is 14 inches. The handler has his dog on SIT-STAY command. He throws a dumbbell over the high jump and, on command, the dog must jump over the high jump, retrieve the dumbbell and return to sit in front of its handler.

Scent Discrimination is a Utility exercise. Five metal and five leather articles are used. The handler's scent is on one of each. The leather article with the handler's scent is placed with the eight other unscented articles, placed approximately 15 feet away and six inches apart. The dog must find and retrieve the scented leather article. The exercise is then repeated with the metal article.

all before age two. For this achievement he received the *Dog World* Award.

Continuing his career, Brandy obtained 100 of the necessary 120 points on the 1981 New England circuit, winning four Highest Scoring Dog in Trial awards and completing his O.T. championship on July 10, 1981.

No. THREE all-time, top winning Shih Tzu bitch, BIS Ch. Zim Shu Van d'Oranje Manege owned by Alan and Lise Miller, was shown by professional handler Wendell Sammet for just nine months. During this short time she won two all-breed Bests in Show, nine Group firsts and 13 other Group placements. She was No. One Shih Tzu Bitch in the United States in 1976. *Ashbey*

No. FOUR all-time, top-winning Shih Tzu bitch in breed competition, BIS Ch. Hoppa Shu V d'Oranje Manege is owned by Alan and Lise Miller and was bred by Eta Pauptit of Holland. Her sire was Hueng Ti of Lhakang and her dam was Ch. Xu Xu Van de Oranje Manege. *Ashbey*

11

The Shih Tzu in the Show Ring

EVERY YEAR, in almost every large community in the United States, there are two, or sometimes more all-breed shows and obedience trials, at which Shih Tzu are eligible to compete. In addition to these, there are many American Shih Tzu Club and affiliate club specialty shows at which only Shih Tzu may be exhibited. Specialty shows offer the same regular classes featured at all-breed shows, and a few non-regular categories, which will be discussed later.

If you bought a Shih Tzu with definite show potential or are thinking about doing so, you should start attending shows in your area and learn all you can about the "gentle" sport of showing dogs. If your puppy was sold to you as a young hopeful, the breeder will not only want you to show it, but will expect you to, providing it developed as the breeder hoped it would and did not fall by the wayside, either because it developed a major fault or because you failed to keep up with its essential socialization and training.

If you bought your puppy purely as a pet, but think it may have become show-worthy, you owe it to the breeder to ask his opinion of your puppy's potential. Breeders want to be just as proud of their puppies in the show ring as you will want to be, and will not want you to show it if it does not reflect the best of his breeding efforts. Either

Ch. Lou Wan Casinova, owned by Wanda Gec was Best in Specialty Show at the ASTC Specialty in St. Louis in 1977. Born on May 13, 1972, he brings forward the genes of some of the great dogs of the Shih Tzu's early days in America to the present through his sire Ch. Mei-Tu of Lou Wan and his dam Fortune Cookie of Lou Wan. To date he is the sire of 15 champions. His pedigree shows five crosses to Ch. Chumulari Ying Ying.

Ashbey

Int. Ch. Bjorneholm's Wu-Ling
Am., Int. Ch. Bjorneholm's Pif
Ranga Ling
Am., Can. Ch. Chumulari Ying Ying
Bjorneholm's Bhadro
Int. Ch. Tangra Von Tschomo-Lungma
Int. Ch. Bjorneholm's Ting-A-Ling

Mei-Tu of Lou Wan

Am., Can. Ch. Chumulari Ying Ying
Chumulari Hai Tao
Chumulari Trari
Ch. Chumulari Ping-Chu
Am., Can. Ch. Chumulari Ying Ying
Chumulari Ching-Fu
Chumulari Dorje

CH. LOU WAN CASINOVA

Int. Ch. Bjornehom's Wu-Ling
Am., Int. Ch. Bjorneholm's Pif
Ranga Ling
Am., Can. Ch. Chumulari Ying Ying
Bjorneholm's Bhadro
Int. Ch. Tangra Von Tschomo-Lungma
Int. Ch. Bjorneholm's Ting-A-Ling

Fortune Cookie of Lou Wan

Am., Can. Ch. Chumulari Ying Ying
Ch. Chumulari Mu Shih
Ch. Katrina of Greenmoss
Ch. Chumulari Mei Mei
Bjorneholm's Bhadro
Ch. Tangra Von Tschomo-Lungma
Int. Ch. Bjorneholm's Ting-A-Ling

186

Every hair is in place on this sensational puppy. Ch. Dragonwyck Miss-B-Havin was just seven months old when she won her first Best in Show. She was bred, owned and handled by Norman L. Patton.

Terri Castellano is another owner-handler who has learned well the art of showing dogs. She is shown here with her homebred, Ali-Aj Diamonds 'N' Frills after taking Winners Bitch and Best of Opposite Sex over champions under the author at Bronx County Kennel Club. She is by Ch. Imua The Gatsby's Pride of Ali-Aj out of Sharn's Chantilly Lace of Ali-Aj.

way, the breeder of your puppy is your best source of information. Otherwise you can buy a dog magazine that lists all the shows, write to The American Kennel Club or call a local all-breed or breed club secretary.

First Impressions

When you enter the show grounds or building you will find yourself in a new, noisy, fascinating world. All appears to be total confusion, yet strangely enough this world is extremely well organized. You will be surrounded on all sides by dogs of different sizes, shapes and colors. You may decide right then and there that showing dogs is not for you but, in case you decide it does look like fun, find out where catalogues of the show are being sold and buy one. It will tell you what breed is being shown in what ring at what time and under what judge. It will list the names of all the dogs entered at this particular show, the names of their sires and dams, the name of the breeder of each dog, the dog's registration number, date of birth and class in which it is entered.

Find out where and when Shih Tzu will be shown and take yourself over to ringside. There you will find breeders and exhibitors either in an area adjoining the ring, grooming their Shih Tzu or, if it is close to ring time, surrounding the ring, brush in hand, ready to put any stray hair back in place.

In general you will find Shih Tzu people warm and friendly, ready to discuss the breed, providing they are not about ready to enter the ring. At that time, they do not welcome a distraction. Otherwise, everyone there, the officials conducting the show, the ring stewards, judges and exhibitors are polite and helpful.

Understanding the Judging

When you attend your first dog show, it will all be rather meaningless unless you have studied what it is all about or accompanied a friend who is able to answer questions.

Each show is an elimination contest, beginning with each different breed competing for the best dog of that breed at that show on that particular day and ending with the ultimate selection of Best Dog in Show.

The Groups and Best in Show

After all breeds have been judged, only one dog of each breed remains undefeated. These undefeated dogs, the Best of Breed and Variety winners, then compete in one of the six different Variety Groups: Sporting, Hound, Working, Terrier, Toy, and Non-Sporting.

At the Ramapo KC show, Lisel's Rock N Rye, handled by his breeder, Lise M. Miller, is awarded Best of Winners from the Bred by Exhibitor Class, while Lisel's Not Coffee but Sanka, is awarded Winners Bitch and Best of Opposite Sex from the classes. She was handled by Dee Shepherd. The judge is Tom Baldwin. Soon after, both "Rocky" and "Sanka" became champions.

Ch. Lisel's Lite N Lively, sister to Ch. Lisel's Eleanor Rigby is pictured after winning Best of Breed from the classes over champion competition at South Shore Kennel Club. She won her first points on September 1, 1979 and completed her championship 28 days later at 13 months of age. Handled by Wendell Sammet, "Lively" was sired by Chumulari Chin Chi out of Ch. Ima Shu van de Oranje Manege.

189

Ch. Truro's The Critic's Choice, owned by Cheryl Crane and Bill Paelko.   *Ashbey*

Ch. Lisel's Eleanor Rigby (Chumulari Chin Chi ex Ima Shu V. d'Oranje Manege), dam of Ch. Lisel's Rock 'N Rye, completed her championship in just 12 shows and never placed below second in the classes.   *Ashbey*

Stylistic Barban Candytuft, bred by Dee Shepherd and Ann Seranne.

Sam Tsus Nefretete, by Ch. Chumulari Chin Te Jih out of Ch. Sam Tsus Maria, bred by Sondra Carroll and owned by Nyle Hansen took a four-point major from the 6–9 month puppy class at Portland KC.

The different breeds within each Group compete for First, Second, Third and Fourth placings and are awarded rosettes, the color of which designates the placement, as in the classes.

At the conclusion of the Group judging, only six dogs remain undefeated, those who took first place in each Group. These finalists compete against each other until one of them is selected as Best in Show. This one dog, at the conclusion of the show, remains undefeated.

Brace and Team Classes

Years ago Brace and Team classes were a part of almost every all-breed show. Today they are rarely offered but, when they are, attract a great deal of spectator enthusiasm.

It seems too bad that these classes are gradually disappearing from the dog show scene. They were an incentive to breeders to aim for uniformity of type. Several large shows encourage entries in the Brace class, but it is years since I have seen a team in action.

A brace is a well-matched pair of the same breed or variety of breed, both owned by the same person or persons and shown side by side. A team is four identical dogs of the same breed, all owned by the same person or persons and shown together. Both a brace or a team may be handled by one or more persons, but are much more spectacular when handled by only one.

I date myself when I admit to the thrill of watching Dr. Vincenzo Calvaresi's legendary team each year at the Westminster Kennel Club show. The tall, trim, graceful Dr. Calvaresi with his quartet of snow-white Maltese with their black sparkling eyes and flowing coats were an unforgettable show in themselves. As he made a sweeping circle down and around the full expanse of the huge Best in Show ring, four leads all in one hand, sixteen small white feet working in unison, he would deliberately let the outside lead slip from his fingers. As the lead trailed behind, the dogs never missed a step. The cheers and applause of the spectators was thunderous.

Naturally, it is easier to produce a matched pair of solid-colored dogs than of bi- or tri-colored ones. In breeds with as wide a variation of colors and markings as our Shih Tzu has, the odds against ever producing a team would be high as the sky. But isn't it nice to imagine the sheer beauty and excitement of four closely matched Shih Tzu taking that same sweep as Dr. Calvaresi's Maltese at an ASTC Specialty? We can dream, can't we?

Specialty Shows

Specialty shows are exactly what the name connotes—or at least should—very special events. They are conducted by a breed club such

191

A well-matched brace is no small achievement in any breed, but is especially difficult with Shih Tzu and the wide variations of colors and markings. First time shown as a brace, these perfectly marked gold and white Shih Tzu went all the way to BEST BRACE IN SHOW. They are Ch. Mandarin's Cinnamon and Ch. Regal's Mark of Excellence, full brothers by Camelot's Beau Brummel out of Mandarin's Sweet N' Sassy. The boys were bred by J. Regelman and Ruth DiNicola, owned by Kris Regelman and shown by Kathy Kwait. *Gilbert*

Am./Can. Ch. Lou Wan Slate of Li Ming was Best of Winners and Best of Opposite Sex at the American Shih Tzu Club Specialty in 1979 under Michele Billings. She was bred by Wanda Gec and Lucretia De Stefano and is owned and handled by Dawn and Robert Tendler. Her sire was Floridonna Flash of Lou Wan and her dam was Ch. Lou Wan Mariposa of Sarifan. *Yuhl*

Ch. Ch'Ang Ch'U Apollo, owned by Tony and Linda Barrand and bred by G. Collins and R. Parker, holds the title in both the United States and Canada. A son of Ch. Dragonwyck The Great Gatsby, this exquisite campaigner took 5-point majors at the ASTC and Trinity Valley Specialties enroute to his title. *Ashbey*

A well-travelled lion dog is Ch. Quang-Te van de Blauwe Mammouth, owned by Rev. and Mrs. D. Allan Easton and bred by the Baroness van Eck-Klasing of Holland. This dog is a world and international champion and also holds titles in Holland, Germany, Belgium, Luxembourg, Canada, Bermuda and the United States. *Ashbey*

Ch. Pinafore Minstrel of Mandarin, owned by Dorothy C. Poole, traces his ancestry back to some of the early greats of the breed. *Ashbey*

The stunning golden dog Ch. Nanjo Avenger is yet another of the many champions sired by Ch. Paisley Ping Pong. This one earned his final points at the Boardwalk KC in 1980

Ch. Yingsu Johnnie Reb achieved fame as a Specialty winner, an all-breed BIS dog and a successful sire. He was bred and is owned by Sue Miller.

Two young titleholders from the Ming Dynasty Kennels are Chs. Fu Manchu and Bamboo Shoot. Photographed at six months, these beauties are by Ch. Jaisu Ling-Ho Chinese Junk ex Barbara's Ming Tu. They were bred and are owned by Gloria Blackburn.

Ch. Lainee Sigmund Floyd, ROM, owned by Elaine Meltzer, established himself early on as a top sire in the breed.

Ch. Chumulari Yu-Lo, owned by Rev. and Mrs. D. Allan Easton, shows the highly desirable black tippings in a gold specimen.

Ch. Jaisu Ling-Ho Chinese Junk, owned by Donna Fritts and bred by Jay Ammon and Carol Walsh, made some outstanding wins including two 5-point Specialty majors. enroute to the title. He is a champion in Canada and the sire of five champions at this writing.

Ch. Bon D'Art Adore Ring of Fancee and Ch. Bon D'Art Amour Ring of Fancee, two stunning sisters that became champions at 14 months in strong Eastern competition. They finished within a day of each other and were owner handled throughout. Bred by Dolly Wheeler and Bonnie Guggenheim, Dori is owned by Marilyn Woodward and Luvi was retained by her breeders.

Ch. Li Ming's Pierre Cardin, pictured at six months of age at his very first show, winning Best of Opposite Sex in the Puppy Sweepstakes a non-regular class held at most Specialty shows as an additional attraction.

Am./Can. Ch. Pen Sans Peaches N' Cream was Winners Bitch at the American Shih Tzu Club National Specialty held at Long Beach, California, June 28, 1979, over a record entry of 81 bitches. Owned by Gloria Busselman, she was sired by Ch. Gold Kung Fu of Tonger out of Nu Sunni Moon of Midhill.   *Yuhl*

193

A BEAUTIFUL MATRON APPEARS AS A VETERAN. Bound to bring tears to the eyes of breeders and exhibitors at a Specialty show are the non-regular Veteran Classes. Pictured is Ch. Golden Elegance of Elfann, beautiful bitch bred by Elfreda Evans and owned by Ruth Di Nicola winning the Veteran Bitch class at the Shih Tzu Club of Northern New Jersey Specialty under Beverly Lehnig. Born in 1970, she was nearly ten years old at the time she made this prestigious win. *Gilbert*

A HANDSOME TRIO. Best Stud Dog at an ASTC Specialty in California is Gardner's Black Devil pictured with two of his get: his son Ch. Bel Air Ace of Spades, owned and handled by Diane Backovich, and his daughter, Ch. San Yen Lai-Dee of the Nite, handled by Kathy Phillips. All three dogs are remarkably similar from the tips of their little black noses to the ends of their well-groomed tails. The judge was Nick Calicura *Yuhl*

as The American Shih Tzu Club or one of its many affiliated clubs throughout the country. They may be held in conjunction with an all-breed show or may be conducted as totally independent affairs. The specialty club usually goes all out with special decorations, an extravagant display of trophies and rosettes, and generous hospitality. Sometimes an official club dinner or cocktail party will be held the evening before the show or at its conclusion.

Parent club specialties are larger and more prestigious events than those of affiliated clubs, and wins at them are considered by most breeders and exhibitors as the ultimate wins of the year. They are the breeder's showcases, and exhibitors often travel many hundreds, even thousands, of miles to attend them.

In addition to the regular classes held at all-breed shows, several non-regular classes may be offered at a specialty club's discretion.

Puppy Sweepstakes

One of the prime attractions of a specialty show is puppy sweepstakes. This is usually judged prior to the regular classes but, sometimes, depending on the size of the show and an estimate of the number of entries, it is done the day before the regular classes are judged.

There are several methods of organizing a sweepstakes. One method is to break the classes down into four categories: Junior dogs, Junior bitches, Senior dogs and Senior bitches. Juniors are puppies six months of age and under nine; senior puppies are nine months of age and under 12 months. First, second, third and fourth placements are selected from each of these classes.

After all four classes have been judged, the first Junior dog competes against first Junior bitch to determine BEST JUNIOR. The same plan is followed in Seniors, and finally, these two compete to determine which puppy is the GRAND PRIZE SWEEPSTAKES WINNER. Sometimes the club will also offer a BEST OF OPPOSITE SEX to the Grand Prize Sweepstakes Winner.

All these wins are coveted and highly prized, although they do not qualify for any points toward a championship.

In addition to a rosette and a trophy, the entry fee is divided among the winners as prize money, a predetermined percentage going to first through fourth placements in each class.

The Veterans

Other popular non-regular classes featured at specialty shows are Veteran Dog and Veteran Bitch. These are for dogs and bitches of a specified age or older, usually six or seven years, depending on the policy of the breed club. Many breeders keep their top-winning cham-

QUITE A SIGHT TO SET BEFORE A JUDGE. An unusual photograph of the Brood Bitch class at the ASTC Specialty in 1977 shows Ch. Mandarin's Royal Rhapsody, R.O.M., handled by Ruth Di Nicola, at the head of the line-up, with five of her offspring in order: Ch. Mandarin's Mischief Maker, Mandarin's Holly, Mandarin's Sugar and Spice, Mandarin's Salt 'N' Pepper and Mandarin's Peaches 'N' Cream. The judge is Edd Embry Bivin.

Petrulis

pions "in coat" to be able to show them in this class at their National Specialty.

Winners of these classes compete against those dogs and bitches entered for Best of Breed competition. Occasionally they win the breed, an honor which is almost always a popular choice with the audience.

Stud Dog Class and Brood Bitch Class

Two other nostalgic non-regular classes, usually offered at Specialty shows, are extras that make a Specialty a truly great event. The Stud Dog class is for sires and two or more of their get, all of which are shown together in the ring. The owner of the Stud Dog need not necessarily be the owner of the get. Similarly Brood Bitches must be shown in the ring with two or more of their produce, and the owner of the bitch need not be the owner of the produce.

Only the quality of the get or produce are to be judged, not the qualities of the Stud Dog or the Brood Bitch.

There are many other innovations that a progressive show chairman can offer at a Specialty to attract additional entries and spectators.

Frequently offered with handsome trophies to the winners are Best Bred by Exhibitor, Best American Bred, Best Puppy in Specialty and Best of Opposite Sex to Best Puppy in Specialty.

And only recently a new class of Junior dogs and bitches has been permitted by the American Kennel Club to be offered at Specialty shows held apart from all-breed events. It is for dogs and bitches whelped in the United States or Canada, at least 12 months of age and not more than 18 months. The purpose is to accomodate those in-betweeners, still puppies at heart but not sufficiently matured to make any great impact in one of the adult classes. It gives exhibitors a chance to enter dogs that are not quite ready for the open class, and should prove to be a popular Specialty show addition.

If you wish to find out where the American Shih Tzu club will be holding future Specialty shows, call or write the American Kennel Club for the name and address of the Club's secretary who will be happy to send you the information.

The parent club's secretary can, in turn, supply you with the name and address of the secretary of an affiliate club in your part of the country.

The Rating Systems—Are they Good or Bad?

Since Irene Schlintz devised and copyrighted "The Phillips System," published for many years in the now-defunct *Popular Dogs Magazine*, almost every dog publication, with the exception of *Pure-Bred Dogs—American Kennel Gazette*, has developed its own rating system or systems.

197

Generally one point is given for each dog defeated by dogs placing in Groups or at Specialty shows. This plan can give so much emphasis to Group and Best in Show wins that it just may be that the tail is wagging the dog!

At the end of a year's duration, the dog accumulating the greatest number of points is announced as TOP DOG, ALL BREEDS. Usually the TOP TEN ALL BREEDS are published followed by the TOP TEN in each of the six groups.

Because of the different cut-off dates and the methods of awarding points, it is not unusual for two different dogs to be claimed NUMBER ONE in a Group or NUMBER ONE ALL BREED, and sometimes neither of them are as good as the dog that earned its championship, owner-handled, over tough competition, judged by highly qualified judges and went home to contribute its qualities to future generations.

The systems mean increased advertising revenue for the magazine or newspaper and additional business for the professional handlers or agents of winners. Unfortunately they also seem to generate a minority group who want to win at any cost to their bank account, their integrity, the well-being and health of their dog or their reputation as breeders and exhibitors. Many real dog people feel strongly that the systems, above the breed level, make crooks out of otherwise honest people, inspire animosities rather than friendships, foster collusion within clubs and take dog shows out of the classification of a sport and place them squarely in the category of a game.

The Top Tenners

So rather than publish the names of the top-winning Group and Best in Show Shih Tzu each year since their official recognition, we thought it might be interesting to find out what Shih Tzu dogs and bitches are the all time top-breed winners.

The figures were immaculately compiled by Lise M. Miller from *American Kennel Gazettes* from January, 1970, when results of the first show at which championship points were awarded to a Shih Tzu were published, through December 1981, or the first eleven years of the Shih Tzu as a recognized breed in the United States.

The number of dogs defeated IN THE BREED and the period of time in which they were shown are also given.

It is interesting to note that almost all the top winners of the breed also won at least one Best in Show. The photographs and pedigrees of many of these dogs can be found in this book.

No. FOUR all-time, top-winning breed winner is Am./Can./Berm. Ch. Winemaker's Pla Boi, shown winning one of his 19 Bests in Show, this one under Judge Robert Graham. Pla Boi was bred, owned and handled by Faye Wine. *Graham*

No. TWO all-time, top-winning dog is BIS Ch. Beedoc Bangaway, bred and owned by Bruna Stubblefield. He was sired by Ch. Beedoc's Ku Che Kuo Want out of Ch. Bel-Air Ms. Erica Beedoc. He is shown with handler Dee Shepherd.

199

Number NINE all-time, top-winning Shih Tzu dog, BIS Ch. Emperor's Thing-A-Ma-Ying was shown from 1974 through 1978. He is pictured winning Best in Show under Mrs. Lucille Meystedt at the Shih Tzu Fanciers of Southern California. By BIS Ch. Chumulari Ying Ying out of Ch. Mar Del's Flutter, he was bred by E.W. Edel and owned by Mrs. Frank Dinelli. His handler was Lesley Boyes. Photo courtesy Rev. and Mrs. D. Allan Easton.

Schley

No. FIVE all-time, top-winning Shih Tzu bitch, Ch. Dalai Razzl Dazzl, owner-handled by his breeder Letz Goodwin, is shown here at 11 months winning Best of Breed over four champions from the 9–12 month puppy class by Mr. Frank Nishimura. She finished in January, 1980 and was then campaigned by Daryl Martin.

Yuhl

No. SIX all-time, top-winning Shih Tzu bitch is BIS Ch. Erincroft Qu Ti Pi of Jasmin owned by Jackie Peterson. She is pictured winning a Toy Group first at ten months under Frank Oberstar. Bred by Geraldine Ikola, Qu Ti Pi finished within a month with two Group 1sts and an all-breed BIS. She was "specialed" for only nine months and was awarded the coveted Elfann Cup for top Best of Opposite Sex Shih Tzu in the United States for 1978. *Ashbey*

```
                                        Int. Ch. Bjorneholm's Pif
                            Ch. Chumulari Ying Ying
                                        Int. Ch. Tangra Von Tschomo-Lungma
                Ch. Dragonwyck The Great Gatsby
                                        Ch. Mariljac Chatterbox
                            Ch. Mariljac Lotus Blossom
                                        Ch. Mariljac Tinkertown Toi
        Can. Ch. Yingsu Lucky Lindy
                                        Ch. Chumulari Ying Ying
                            Ch. Chumulari Chung Hsia Te
                                        Chumulari Trari
                Can. Ch. Gin Doc's Pocahanas
                                        Ch. Golden Oscar
                            Peersun's Evening Ember
                                        Bambu Tibetan Blossom
CH. ERINCROFT QU TI PI OF JAZMIN
                                        Ch. Si Shu v.d. Oranje Manege
                            Ch. Parquin's Sarrtezza
                                        Lakoya's Lu Lu
                Ch. Parquin's Pretty Boy Floyd
                                        Ch. Parquin's Sarrtezza
                            Indian Magic of Parquin's
                                        Parquin's Cassim
        Yingsu Soy Sauce
                                        Ch. Chumulari Ying Ying
                            Ch. Chumulari Chung Hsia Te
                                        Chumulari Trari
                Can. Ch. Gin Doc's Pocahanas
                                        Ch. Golden Oscar
                            Peersun's Evening Ember
                                        Bambu Tibetan Blossom
```

The Top Tenners

Rank	Dog's Name	(Breed Only) No. Dogs Beaten	Years Shown
1.	BIS Ch. Dragonwyck The Great Gatsby	3496	1975 to 1979
2.	BIS Ch. Beedoc's Bangaway	2331	1978 to 1981
3.	BIS Ch. Afshi's Gunther	2073	1976 to 1979
4.	BIS Ch. Winemaker's Plai Boi	2000	1974 to 1977
5.	BIS Ch. House of Wu Hai Yu	1774	1975 to 1979
6.	BIS Ch. Hullabaloo Jay Ray of Nanjo	1757	1975 to 1979
7.	BIS Ch. Chumulari Chin Tzu Jih	1628	1976 to 1978
9.	BIS Ch. Emperor's Thing-A-Ma-Ying	1491	1974 to 1979
8.	BIS Ch. Ying Su Johnny Reb	1506	1979 to 1980
10.	BIS Ch. Aagalyn I'm a Dandi	1119	1973 to 1978

Rank	Bitch's Name	(Breed Only) No. Dogs Beaten	Years Shown
1.	BIS Ch. Witch's Wood Yum Yum	3112	1971 through 1975
2.	BIS Ch. Ah So Su Suki	1918	1978 to 1981
3.	BIS Ch. Zim Shu v. d Oranje Manege*	939	9 months only 1975 to 1976
4.	BIS Ch. Hoppa Shu v. d Oranje Manege	881	1976 through 1977
5.	Ch. Dalai Razzle Dazzle	879	1980 through 1981
6.	BIS Erincroft Qu-Ti-Pi of Jasmin	575	1977 through 1978
7.	BIS & BISS Char-Nick Bewitching of Copa	560	1974 to 1975
8.	BIS Ch. Tipton's Jen-Mi	537	1975 through 1976
9.	BIS Gin Doc's Suzy of Sanquish	533	1976 through 1977
10.	BISS Ch. Luken's All-Fired Up	524	1980 through 1981

*Top breed winner in one AKC reported Year.

Junior Showmanship

Most all-breed shows offer classes in Junior Showmanship competition and there usually are four classes: Novice Junior and Senior, and Open Junior and Senior.

Novice Junior Class is for boys and girls at least ten and under thirteen years of age who have never won a first place in this class at a licensed show.

Novice Senior is for boys and girls at least ten and under seventeen years of age who have never won a first place in this class at a licensed show.

Top Junior Handler of Shih Tzu for 1978 and 1979, Brent Meidlinger is pictured winning Best Junior Handler at the 1979 ASTC Specialty in Southern California with Escort Billy Bud of Mei San.

Brent's sister, Brenda Meidlinger, got Ch. Mai San Hey Checker Over when she was just a pup, trained her and showed her both in Junior Showmanship and also in the breed ring, where "Checker" earned her championship points and a few placings in the Group.

203

Open Junior Class is for boys and girls at least ten and under thirteen years of age who HAVE won a first place in Novice Junior Class at a licensed show.

Open Senior Class is for boys and girls at least thirteen and under seventeen years of age who HAVE won a first place in Novice Senior Class at a licensed show.

The winner of each Novice class is automatically eligible to enter and compete in the corresponding Open class at the show.

Children are usually first introduced to the world of showing dogs at match shows where any age may participate and gain the necessary experience to compete in point shows. Along the way they gain in poise and confidence, learn how to dress and to become good sports. They are taught that ungroomed hair and sloppy clothes will count against them. They learn to shake hands with the winner and to take their wins and losses alike without bragging or resentment.

The competition at point shows is rough, and to win the juniors have to be good. Once bitten by the show bug, they usually try to attend as many weekend shows as possible in order to win the necessary first placements to qualify them for Junior Showmanship at the Westminster Kennel Club in February. Children come from all areas of the country to this show in the hope of taking the honors, while encouragement from thousands of spectators add excitement to the event.

Many successful Junior Showmanship alumni find their life's work in the dog world, as handlers, trainers or judges.

Brother-Sister Team

Brent Meidlinger began showing dogs when he was 13 years old with a dog named Mei San Ruffian who was a poor dog conformation-wise, but a good showman nonetheless. They started in the Novice Senior class as one of the youngest teams. Before long Ruffian and Brent were placing at nearly every show. Soon Ruffian was replaced by a better-quality dog, but wins were hard to come by because dog and handler did not work well together.

Finally, in 1978, Brent bought a puppy from his mother and trained him when he was very young. A son of Ch. Lou Wan's Casinova, Escort's Billy Bud of Mei San matured into a lovely Shih Tzu and this was the turning point in Brent's Junior Showmanship career. Billy was flashy and never quit showing. They worked perfectly as a team and Billy and Brent began winning almost everytime they stepped into the ring.

Although judges are supposed to judge the handler and not the dog, Brent feels that a lot of judges put too much emphasis on how the dog shows and not on how the handler shows the dog. He advises children interested in exhibiting in Junior Showmanship to "get a flashy young puppy that has a lot of spunk and natural showmanship and train it. When it matures you'll have the perfect blend of handler and dog."

Brenda Meidlinger, Brent's sister, first entered Novice Junior Showmanship at a fun match about six years ago. Her mother suggested it might be fun for her. She didn't really know what to do or what was expected of her, but won a third place ribbon. From that time on she was hooked. Brenda thinks that, "Junior Showmanship is important to young people, because it prepares them for breeding; it teaches them to win and lose gracefully and not to take a loss personally, knowing there will be many more shows and many other judges."

Brenda feels it is very important for the junior to have a dog that is good enough to compete in the breed ring. "The dog should always be clean and the handler dressed nicely—not in jeans and a T-shirt."

Some very lovely Shih Tzu are bred and owned in Canada. Am./Can. Ch. Ch'Ang Ch'U Apollo shows a remarkable likeness to his famous sire, BIS Ch. Dragonwyck The Great Gatsby. Out of Ch. Li Ming's Ameretta, he was bred by G. Collins and R. Parker and is owned by Mr. and Mrs. Barrand in Canada. "Apollo" acquired his American title, owner-handled in four consecutive shows, going Best of Winners each time. He won five-point majors at both the parent and Trinity Valley Specialties.   *Ashbey*

Int. Ch. Bjorneholm's Pif

Ch. Chumulari Ying Ying

Int. Ch. Tangra Von Tschomo-Lungma

Ch. Dragonwyck The Great Gatsby

Ch. Mariljac Chatterbox

Ch. Mariljac Lotus Blossom

Ch. Mariljac Tinkertown Toi

AM., CAN. CH. CH'ANG CH'U APOLLO

Ch. Dragonwyck The Great Gatsby

Ch. Imua The Gatsby's Pride of Ali Aj, C.D.

Ch. Imua's Wicked Wahine

Ch. Li Ming's Ameretta

Ch. Lou Wan Casinova

Ch. Li Ming's Po Lo Mi

Ch. Tienchao's San Se Chin

206

12

The Shih Tzu in Canada

LONG BEFORE Shih Tzu were recognized in the United States, Canadians were deeply involved in the breed. Throughout the years the Canadian breeders have made steady progress in improving both coat quality and conformation, borrowing heavily from lines in the United States when they felt it necessary.

Shih Tzu are shown in the Non-Sporting Group in Canada, and at Group level the competition is much tougher than in the Canadian Toy Group. In Non-Sporting, the Shih Tzu must hold its own against such formidable rivals as the Poodle, the Lhasa Apso and the Chow Chow so a mediocre dog in Canada can end up at the bottom of the pile just as fast as in the States, and often faster. Stateside exhibitors are inclined to think they can take just any old thing up to Canada and "clean up," but without a really good dog, they will usually come home sadder, wiser and "well-trounced!"

Canadian breeders for the most part do not operate on as large a scale as those in the United States, breeding only a few litters each year. Owners generally show their own dogs, although there are some excellent Canadian professional handlers who have demonstrated their expertise in presenting Shih Tzu.

Everyone should experience the ambience of Canadian shows at least once in a lifetime. And when you go, be prepared to learn. Instead of idle gossip around ringside, you will find people who are intensely

BIS Ch. Samalee's Reflections of Baron, a lovely gold and white Canadian-bred, shown winning Best of Breed over 36 champions under judge Gilbert Kahn in a total entry of 144, the largest ever in Canada. A combination of Mar-Del and Winemaker lines, Baron is owned by Ron and Marnie (handling) Oystrick.

Multiple BIS Am./Can. Ch. Imua's Guava Jam wins Best Stud Dog over an entry of nine at the Canadian Shih Tzu Club Specialty in 1979 under Gilbert Kahn.

Ch. Samalee's Precious Golden Girl shares the limelight with Ch. Samalee's Reflections of Baron, winning Best of Opposite Sex at the 1979 National Specialty under judge Gilbert Kahn and completing her championship at the same time. "Precious," from an all-champion litter of three, os owned and shown by Marnie Oystrick in Canada. *Weston*

And the delightful Brood Bitch (Female in Canada) class at that same specialty was won by Ch. Copa's Cherish of Samalee pictured with litter sisters Ch. Samalee's Precious Golden Girl and Ch. Samalee's Crystal Mint, bred and owned by Ron and Marnie Ostrick. "Cherish" was sired by BIS Am./Can. Ch. Aagalynn's I'm A Dandy out of Amilou's Shesadandi and was owner-handled.

209

interested and you will hear constructive criticism. Take along your best Shih Tzu and be prepared to meet up with some very fine competition.

Canadian Show of Shows

In late fall of each year when the show season is over, the Ottawa Kennel Club presents an extravaganza known as "The Show of Shows," where only those dogs which have won an all-breed Best in Show award under Canadian Kennel Club rules throughout that year are eligible to compete.

Dogs compete only in their respective Groups, and only one winner in each group is selected—Number One.

Five all-breed judges officiate at each of these unique shows.

Each Group and the Best in Show is judged by three judges, whose names are selected at random from a hat containing the names of all five judges. The names are drawn after all dogs are assembled in the ring and just prior to the commencement of the judging. In this way no one knows which three of the judges will be evaluating his entry and the judges themselves do not know what Group or Groups will be allotted to them by chance.

Each judge scores the dogs out of a possible ten points, and the score cards are tabulated by a disinterested person. The dog receiving the highest number of points is the winner of the Group. Best Dog in Show is selected in the same manner. In case of a tie, the two additional judges are called into the ring to add their scores and, hopefully, break the tie.

Shih Tzu Wins 1971 Show of Shows

A captivating little Shih Tzu named Choo Lang of Telota, an American and Canadian champion, sashayed off with top honors in some of the hottest competition Canadians have ever seen in the show ring.

There were more than fifty dogs from across Canada and the United States assembled at the 1971 "Show of Shows," many were multiple Best in Show winners in both countries.

The ringside was packed with spectators as the judges were introduced. They were Mrs. Edna Joel, Mrs. Ena Stewart, Mr. John Devlin, Mr. Theodore Gundersen, and Mr. John Murphy.

The excitement mounted to a climax when two dogs tied for the honors in both the Working and the Toy Groups, and a fraction of a point decided the winner in each case, by the two extra judges. Choo Lang's competition was the lovely Maltese, Ch. Pendleton's Jewel owned by Dorothy and Norman White of Youngstown, Ohio.

The names of Mrs. Stewart, Mrs. Joel, and Mr. Devlin were drawn

Canadian Ch. Nanking Mari Melody, bred, owned and shown by Mrs. Gerry Ikola. Melody was sired by Am. Ch. Mariljac Maripet out of Cabrand's Ciara of Lou Wan, whose grandsire was also Maripet.

Int. Ch. Bjorneholm's Wu-Ling — Nord. Ch. Bjorneholm's Tsemo / Nord. Ch. Bjorneholm's Lulu

Int. Ch. Bjorneholm's Pif

Ranga Ling — Ch. Wang-Ling / Ch. Ang Lahmu

Ch. Chumulari Ying Ying

Bjorneholm's Bhadro — Ch. Bjorneholm's Tu-Tu / Bjorneholm's Fie

Int. Ch. Tangra Von Tschomo-Lungma

Int. Ch. Bjorneholm's Ting-A-Ling — Ch. Bjorneholm's Wu-Ling / Ch. Bjorneholm's Bolette

Ch. Mariljac Maripet

Int. Ch. Bjorneholm's Wu-Ling — Nord. Ch. Bjorneholm's Tsemo / Nord. Ch. Bjorneholm's Lulu

Int. Ch. Bjorneholm's Pif

Ranga Ling — Ch. Wang-Ling / Ch. Ang Lahmu

Mariljac Cha Boom

Jungfaltets Wu-Po — Lhipoiang / Jungfaltets Jung Wu-Pi

Mariljac Monsey Bonsey Colwell

Si Kiang's Mi Tzi — Si Kiang's Bamsy Wamsy / Pukedal's Ai-Lan

CAN. CHS. NANKING MARI MELODY and MARI-LU TAMAWAE

Ch. Mar-Del's Chow Mein — Jungfaltets Wu-Po / Si Kiang's Mi Tzi

Ch. Mar-Del's Ring-A-Ding-Ding

Ch. Mar-Del's Snow Pea — Jungfaltets Wu-Po / Si Kiang's Madame Wu

Ch. Paisley Ping Pong

Ch. Mar-Del's Chow Mein — Jungfaltets Wu-Po / Si Kiang's Mi Tzi

Ch. Paisley Petronella

Pitti-Sing of Sangchen — Kwan Yen Wu Tu of Sangchen / Ling Ling of Sangchen

Cabrand's Ciara of Lou Wan

Ch. Chumulari Ying Ying — Int. Ch. Bjorneholm's Pif / Int. Ch. Tangra Von Tschomo-Lungma

Ch. Mariljac Maripet — Int. Ch. Bjorneholm's Pif / Mariljac Monsey Bonsey Colwell

Mariljac Cha Boom

Cabrand's Cara of Lou Wan

Ch. Chumulari Ying Ying — Int. Ch. Bjorneholm's Pif / Int. Ch. Tangra Von Tschomo-Lungma

Fortune Cookie of Lou Wan

Ch. Chumulari Mei Mei — Ch. Chumulari Mu Shih / Int. Ch. Tangra Von Tschomo-Lungma

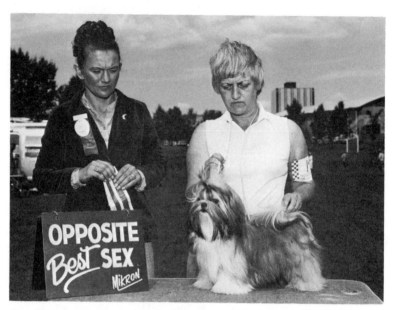

Can. Ch. Luvncare Cherry Red, bred, owned and handled by Rosemarie Hoo, one of Canada's leading breeders, is pictured winning Winners Female (the word bitch is not used in Canada), and Best of Opposite Sex over two champions. She was sired by Can. Ch. Imua's Director of Luvncare out of Can. Ch. Mar-Del's Ring Ling.

Mik Ron

Most Canadian competitors are owner-handlers. The few who show other people's dogs professionally are proficient at their work. Garrett Lambert is one of these, pictured here winning BIS under Winifred Heckmann with Ch. Carrimount Ah Chun-Ki, bred by Jeffrey Carrique and owned by Heather Johnstone. Out of Can. Ch. Carrimount Ah-Chou-Chou by Am./Can. Ch. Greenmoss Golden Frolic of Elfann, Chun-Ki's record includes one all-breed Canadian BIS and one Canadian Specialty Best. A Group winner in both United States and Canada, he is from an all-champion litter of five.

212

Am./Can. Ch. Wynn Dee's Cheerleader of Ho Chi, is owned by Betty Meidlinger and was bred by Linda Miller. She is pictured being awarded Best of Winners at Brantford, Ontario under Joan Morden. The handler is Betty Nissen.

BIS Am. Can. Ch. Strawberry Blond Luvncare, handled by Emily Gunning, was Best Puppy in Show at KARS under James Taylor. Bred by J. Beath and owned at that time by Rosemarie Hoo, this superstar puppy finished her Canadian championship in three days with two Group firsts, and two Best Puppy in Show wins at eleven months. Her sire was BIS Am./Can. Ch. Imua's Guava Jam and her dam was Can. Ch. Sun Chine Loli Pop. *Wibaut*

213

from the hat to officiate in the Best in Show ring, and Choo Lang shown by his co-owner and handler, William Guzzy, was announced the ultimate winner.

It was the first time in the show's history that all six finalists were owned by Americans.

Canadian Breeders

Canadians, like their English cousins, are instinctively good breeders. In developing the qualities of the Shih Tzu in Canada, they line bred intelligently to magnify and retain the best qualities, outcrossing only when necessary and always for a good reason.

The Story of Ch. Yingsu Lucky Lindy

Can. Ch. Yingsu Lucky Lindy, a lovely gold and white Shih Tzu male, was bred by Sue Miller in Greer, South Carolina, and owned by Mrs. Gerry Ikola of Hillsburgh, Ontario.

Born on September 9, 1975, Lindy lost his life 4½ years later, when he fell through thin ice far out in the middle of a pond. All rescue attempts failed to save him.

His tragic death was a true loss to the Shih Tzu breed in America but, fortunately, Lindy left behind him a legacy of some of the greatest Shih Tzu precursors, through his 12 champion get—six American and six Canadian.

```
                              Int. Ch. Bjorneholm's Pif
                  Ch. Chumulari Ying Ying
                                Int. Ch. Tangra Von Tschomo Lungma
          Ch. Dragonwyck The Great Gatsby
                          Ch. Mariljac Chatterbox
              Ch. Mariljac Lotus Blossom
                            Ch. Mariljac Tinkertown Toi
    CH. YINGSU LUCKY LINDY
                              Ch. Chumulari Ying Ying
              Ch. Chumulari Chung Hsia Te
                    Chumulari Trari
          Ch. Gin Doc's Pocohanas
                        Ch. Golden Oscar
              Peersun's Evening Ember
                        Bambu Tibetan Blossom
```

BIS Can. Ch. Gralee Jokers R Wild, pictured winning Best in Show at 12 months of age. Sired by Can. Ch. Paramount Lucky Lin Chu out of Ch. Yingsu Bren Dee Lee of Gra Lee, Lindy's sister, he was bred by Leslie Sherratt and is owned by Frank and Lynda McClymont. "Joker," a prepotent sire, is carrying on where Lindy left off.

<pre>
                                      Ch. Dragonwyck The Great Gatsby
                    Ch. Yingsu Lucky Lindy
                                      Ch. Gin Doc's Pocohanas
          Ch. Paramount Lucky Lin Chu
                                      Ch. Parquin's Pretty Boy Floyd
                    Yingsu Nyith Kwong Ming
                                      Ch. Gin Doc's Pocohanas
CAN. CH. GRALEE VEGAS JOKERS R WILD
                                      Ch. Chumulari Ying Ying
                    Ch. Dragonwyck The Great Gatsby
                                      Ch. Mariljac Lotus Blossom
          Ch. Yingsu Bren Dee Lee of Gralee
                                      Ch. Chumulari Chung Hsia Te
                    Ch. Gin Doc's Pocohanas
                                      Peersun's Evening Ember
</pre>

A STAR IS BORN. The pictures on these pages show a puppy's development from seven to twenty months. He is Can. Ch. Shente's Brandy Alexander, bred and owned by Margaret Brown and handled by Luke Ehricht.

Brandy wins Best Puppy in Group at his very first show under Wally Bowden. He was just seven months old at the time.   *Stonham*

At ten months, Brandy won 5 points from the puppy class to complete his Canadian championship under Morley Thornton.   *Weston Photography*

216

After seven months of retirement to mature and grow coat, Brandy makes his first appearance in the Canadian show ring as a champion, and wins BEST IN SHOW under Joseph Gregory. *Weston Photography*

```
                                    Char Nick's Mr. Chan
                        Ch. Char Nick's I Gotcha
                                    Pakos Lotus Blossom
              Ch. Nanjo's Oh Mai Gosh of Char Nick
                                    Ch. Char Nick's Sam Chu
                        Ch. Char Nick's Sesame of Sam Chu
                                    Char Nick's Kwan Yen Tzu
       Ch. Afshi's Gunther
                                    Ch. Mar-Del's Ring-A-Ding-Ding
                        Ch. Paisley Ping Pong
                                    Ch. Paisley Petronella
              Afshi's Tekhla
                                    Ch. Mar-Del's Chow Mein
                        Ch. Emperor's Adoring Amah
                                    Aagalyn's Water Chestnut
CAN. CH. SHENTE'S BRANDY ALEXANDER
                                    Ch. Mar-Del's Chow Mein
                        Ch. Mar-Del's Ring-A-Ding-Ding
                                    Ch. Mar-Del's Snow Pea
              Ch. Charjalong's Bronze Bandit
                                    Ch. Carrimount Ah Chop Chop
                        Ch. Long's Heide Ho Ah Chop Chop
                                    Ch. Long's Little Lick
       Sharn's Rising Star
                                    Ch. Mar-Del's Ring-A-Ding-Ding
                        Ch. Paisley Ping Pong
                                    Ch. Paisley Petronella
              Ch. Char Nick's Star of Sharn
                                    Ch. Si Kiang's Jody's Tidbie Toodle
                        Ch. Char Nick's Sam-Fu-Li-Po
                                    Si Kiang's Prci-Phe
```

217

Reaching his full potential in coat abundance and showmanship, Brandy took his second all-breed Best in Show at 20 months of age under James Taylor.   *Wibaut*

Before he was 22 months old, Brandy accumulated a total of three all-breed Bests in Show, one Best in a National Specialty, six Group firsts and 18 other Group placements.

Am. & Can. Ch. Shente's Mr. MacBarker, C.D. (Can. Ch. Fang Chu's Lipton Chee ex Can. Ch. MissTiss Tzuzzie Q of Chu Ling, Can. C.D.) owned by John Hollingsworth, was Best Puppy in Breed at the Canadian National Sportsmen's Show in 1979.

Sire of "Strawberry Blond" is the handsome Am./Can. BIS Ch. Imua's Guava Jam. He was top-winning male Shih Tzu in Canada in 1979 and his wins include 12 Group firsts. In 1978 he was Best of Winners at Westminster and in 1979 won the Stud Dog class at the Canadian Specialty. The sire of nine champions, he was bred by Ginger Schedlbauer and is owned by Rosemarie Hoo.

"Joker" is the sire of Can. Ch. Vegas Star Attraction, carrying on the family tradition by winning Best Puppy in Show at eight months of age. "Star" is handled by his breeder-owner, Lynda McClymont. "Joker" has two other Canadian Champions and three more get are pointed as this book goes to press.

Litter sister to "Precious," Ch. Samalee's Crystal Mint finished her championship under Quentin LaHam. The all champion litter was sired by BIS Am. Ch. Kee-Lee's Red Baron of Mar-Del out of Ch. Copa's Cherish of Samalee. It was bred, owned and shown by Ron and Marnie Oystrick of Ontario, Canada.

Lindy was a large dog, so Gerry wisely bred him to Maripet to introduce a smaller type, without going too far away from her original line. Lindy's grandsire and Maripet's sire was the same dog, the well-known Ch. Chumulari Ying Ying. Bred to his half sisters, Yingsu Soy Sauce, owned by Sue Miller, and Yingsu Nyth Kwong Ming, owned by Diane Moncion, he produced a line of super movers. Ming and Soy Sauce had the same dam as Lindy and their sire was Ch. Pretty Boy Floyd. Ming also died a tragic death from heat prostration at age four.

Lindy was No. 4 Top Shih Tzu producer in the United States in 1979 and tied for Top Producer in Canada in 1978. He sired 1979's Top Shih Tzu in the United States, BIS Ch. Paramount MGM Dragonwyck, bred by Diane Moncion, and BIS Ch. Erincroft Qu Ti Pi of Jazmin, bred by Jerry Ikola and owned by Jack Peterson. Lindy's sister, Yingsu Bren Dee Lee of Gra Lee also produced a Best in Show winner.

Two of Lindy's Grandsons won the breed and also Best of Winners at the 1979 ASTC Specialty. They were Ch. Yingsu Johnie Reb, owned by Sue Miller, and Ch. Jazmin's Maximillion, owned by Jackie Peterson.

The amazing part of these accomplishments is that Lindy did them all by four years of age, and by siring just a very few special litters each year.

The Canadian Shih Tzu Club

The Shih Tzu has a parent club in Canada, just as it has a parent club in the United States, and there are several affiliated clubs across the breadth of the Canadian Provinces, which give yearly Specialties and match shows.

For further information about these clubs, their specific location, and names of their Secretaries, write or phone the Canadian Kennel Club.

BIS Ch. Yingsu's Johnie Reb, pictured winning one of his many Best of Breed awards. He was one of the youngest dogs to win the National Specialty, prevailing in May 1979 at just 18 months old. Handled by Emily Gunning, he was bred and is owned by Sue Miller.

```
                      Ch. Chumulari Ying Ying              Int. Ch. Bjorneholm's Pif
          Ch. Dragonwyck The Great Gatsby                  Int. Ch. Tangra V. Tscomo-Lungm
                    Ch. Mariljac Lotus Blossom             Ch. Mariljac Chatterbox
          Can. Ch. Yingsu's Lucky Lindy                    Ch. Mariljac Tinkertown Toi
                      Ch. Chumulari Chung Hsia Te          Ch. Chumulari Ying Ying
    ┌Can. Ch. Gin Doc's Pocohanas                          Chumulari Trari
    │                 Peersun's Evening Ember              Ch. Golden Oscar
Erincroft Double O Seven                                   Bambu Tibetan Blossom
                      Ch. Parquin's Sartezza               Ch. Si Shu v.d. Oranje Manege
          Ch. Parquin's Pretty Boy Floyd                   Lakoya's Lu Lu
                      Indian Magic of Parquin's            Ch. Parquin's Sarrtezza
    Yingsu's Soy Sauce                                     Parquin's Cassim
                      Ch. Chumulari Chung Hsia Te          Ch. Chumlari Ying Ying
    └Can. Ch. Gin Doc's Pocohanas                          Chumulari Trari
                      Peersun's Evening Ember              Ch. Golden Oscar
CH. YINGSU'S JOHNNIE REB                                   Bambu Tibetan Blossom
                     ┌Ch. Lyckobringardens Guy of Vita Hund  Ch. Templegardens Chi-Co-Tzu
          Ch. Vita Hund's Hsien-Sheng, C.D.                Ch. Amulett-Yin
                     │Ch. Vita Hund's Hsi-Wang             Ch. Anibes Satru
          Mei-Hua Ti Adversary                             Ch. Chumulari P'eng Yu
                     │Gwehelog Kong Ming                   Kulu of Golvale
          Can. Ch. Mei-Hua Mai Minh of Leistraum, C.D.X.  Bluemarkings Melody
                     │Seng Fu's Dol-Li of Leistraum        Mogene's Fanfare
    Can. Ch. Mei-Hua Elegance of Yingsu                    Mogene's T. Ho-Ping
                     │Ch. Anibes Satru                     Ch. Anibes Cris-Pin
          Vita Hund's Ming-Jen                             Bjorneholms Peyssy
                     │Ch. An-Ge-Lih                        Ch. Templegardens Chi-Co-Tzu
          Vita Hund's Niu-Tzu of Mei-Hua                   Bey-The-Wang
                     └Ch. Lyckobringardens Guy of Vita Hund  Ch. Templegardens Chi-Co-Tzu
          Vita Hund's Mei-Kung-Chu                         Ch. Amulett-Yin
                      Ch. An-Ge-Lih                        Ch. Templegardens Chi-Co-Tzu
                                                           Bey-The-Wang
```

13

The Inheritance of Coat
Color in the Shih Tzu

THE MANNER in which color genes are transmitted from one generation to another, is a real challenge to the breeder, especially in view of the fact that many geneticists don't agree on how various colors are transferred and why some dilute with age while others have staying power.

Extensive studies have been made in some breeds to determine the mode of transference, but little controlled experimentation has been done with the Shih Tzu. This seems a shame since the variety of colors and markings make it a natural for the scientist. The breed offers a kaleidescope of colors, shades, hues and intensities from the delicate pastels to the vibrant dark tones with great variation in the distribution of white and color on the body. Certainly no book on the Shih Tzu would be complete without a chapter devoted to this highly complex subject.

However, I am going to try to deal with it as simply as possible, using words that are familiar to all.

Sometimes I think that scientists go out of their way to try to confuse and complicate a subject by the use of unfamiliar, Latin-derived terms, making it difficult to understand when in actuality, and with a dictionary by one's side, it is relatively simple. In dealing with color genes, our scientists came up with the delicious words, EPISTATIC

223

Ch. Lou Wan's The Great Houdini is an excellent example of close linebreeding to a great dog. It is necessary to go back to the fifth generation to see how closely linebred he is to Ch. Chumulari Ying Ying and Ch. Bjorneholm's Ting a Ling. Notice how carefully the breeders have brought forward these dogs of the past into the present. Both the sire and the dam of Houdini's sire are the result of half-brother, half-sister breedings. But the stage was carefully set before this inbreeding was attempted.

CH. LOU WAN THE GREAT HOUDINI

Int. Ch. Bjorneholm's Pif
Ch. Chumulari Ying Ying
Int.-Ch. Tangra Von Tschomo-Lungma
Ch. Mei Tu of Lou Wan
Chumulari Hai Tao
Ch. Chumulari Ping Chu
Chumulari Ching-Fu
Ch. Lou Wan Casinova
Int. Ch. Bjorneholm's Pif
Ch. Chumulari Ying Ying
Int. Ch. Tangra Von Tschomo-Lungma
Fortune Cookie of Lou Wan
Chumulari Mu Shih
Ch. Chumulari Mei Mei
Int. Ch. Tangra Von Tschomo-Lungma

Ch. Mei Tu of Lou Wan
Ch. Cabrand's Lou Wan v. Alarickhan
Fortune Cookie of LouWan
Walden's Ezekiel
Chumulari Di Di

Rondelay Chile of Lou Wan
Rondelay Polli Ana
Lou Wan Melinda
Ch. Chumulari Sheng Li Che
Chumulari Ling Hsui
Chumulari Dorje
Pekoe of Lou Wan
Chumulari Di Di

Rondelay Chile of Lou Wan
Rondelay Polli Ana

Int. Ch. Bjorneholm's Wu-Ling
Ranga Ling
Bjorneholm's Bhadro
Int. Ch. Bjorneholm's Ting-A-Ling
Ch. Chumulari Ying Ying
Chumulari Trari
Ch. Chumulari Ying Ying
Chumulari Dorje
Int. Ch. Bjorneholm's Wu-Ling
Ranga Ling
Bjorneholm's Bhadro
Int. Ch. Bjorneholm's Ting-A-Ling
Ch. Chumulari Ying Ying
Ch. Katrina of Greenmoss
Bjorneholm's Bhadro
Int. Ch. Bjorneholm's Ting-A-Ling
Ch. Chumulari Ying Ying
Ch. Chumulari Ping Chu
Ch. Chumulari Ying Ying
Ch. Chumulari Mei Mei
Chumulari Mu Shih
Int. Ch. Tangra Von Tschomo-Lungma
Si Kiang's Tashi
Mistybank Houdini
Ch. Chumulari Ying Ying
Chumulari Trari
Jungfaltets Wu-Po
Chumulari Trari
Chumulari Mu Shih
Int. Ch. Tangra Von Tschomo-Lungma
Si Kiang's Tashi
Mistybank Houdini

and HYPOSTATIC to describe the order of the expression of a specific group of genes where one quality masks another. These are nothing more or less than DOMINANT and RECESSIVE respectively in varying degrees.

But we're getting ahead of ourselves.

First, we must understand that there are only two major types of pigment—DARK and BLOND or TAN, and there are at least TEN MAJOR GENES involved in the expression of color, both the quality and quantity of color, and its intensity.

SIX of the gene pairs work strictly in accordance with Mendelian principles, producing two qualities, the dominant one capable of masking the recessive one. FOUR of the gene pairs are a series, producing more than two usual qualities. These are known as ALLELES. They are situated at one location or loci on the chromosome and make it possible for the inheritance of a varying degree of a quality. These degrees or alleles have an order of dominance to each other similar to the "pecking order."

An ALLELE (pronounced *a-leel*) or an ALLELOMORPH is an alternative form of the same gene, which influences the same characteristic in a dog but in different ways. EPISTATIC is the masking of one factor by another not allelomorphic to it, or in more familiar terms, DOMINANT. HYPOSTATIC denotes a hidden factor, masked by another that is not an allelomorph—or RECESSIVE to it.

A PAIR is straight dominant-recessive Mendelian in expression.

A SERIES has more than one pair of alleles.

The Inheritance of Coat Color in Dogs

Clarence D. Little, Director Emeritus of the Jackson Memorial Laboratory, at Bar Harbour, Maine, is by all means the most advanced and knowledgeable scientist on color transference and his book, *The Inheritance of Coat Color in Dogs*, is a valuable and authoritative work on the subject. But Dr. Little makes suppositions that are certainly questionable.

When basing his theories and conclusions on his own experiments, no one can argue with him but, in breeds where he depended on exhibitors who were not true breeders to supply him with the necessary data, he bogs down badly into the mire of genetic confusion and contradiction. The Yorkshire Terrier is one breed where he goofs badly. The desirable blue body coat, which it contributed to the Silky Terrier, is not the "clerical grey" or pewter shades caused by the dilution of black. It is more likely to be a double gg recessive, but that is another story.

After studying Mr. Little's book for weeks and feeling very much

225

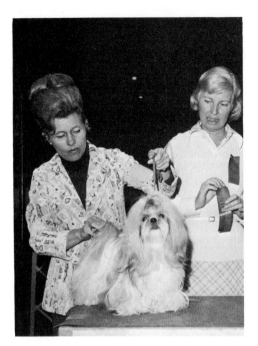

Am./Can. Ch. Greenmoss Gilligan, sired Ch. Winemaker's Pla Boi and two other Best in Show offspring. Ch. Winemaker's Candi Man, won a Best in Show in Canada, and a daughter earned her Best in Show in Japan. *Graham*

Ch. Winemaker's Stormee Night, bred and owned by Faye Wine and Gay Prellaman was judged Best at the ASTC Specialty in Miami in January, 1981. *Graham*

226

lost among the allelomorphs, it is thanks to Major Barre Hasle, of Norway, who wrote a series of articles in the *Shih Tzu News* in 1975, entitled "Seeking the Blues," that comprehension of color genes began to dawn and the sun came shining through the clouds of confusion.

The Color Genes

Remind yourself constantly that there are only TWO BASIC TYPES OF PIGMENT—DARK and BLONDE (or tan, sandy, yellow, sable, red).

The ten genes definitely known to be involved in color transference are:

The *A*-Gene Series
The *B*-Gene Pair
The *C*-Gene Series
The *D*-Gene Pair
The *E*-Gene Series
The *G*-Gene Pair
The *M*-Gene Pair
The *P*-Gene Pair
The *S*-Gene Series
The *T*-Gene Pair

If we only have two types of pigment, DARK and BLONDE, where does white come in?

Basically, a different gene determines whether or not the two major types of pigment will retreat from a specific area to allow those areas to become white. We will deal more with the subject of white when we come to the *C*-Gene Series.

First let us see how Major Borre Haise groups the ten color genes in logical fashion:

S and *T* are the white determiners
M and *P* are the special effects determiners
B and *D* are the special color determiners
C and *G* are strength determiners
A and *E* are the color and pattern determiners

The A-Gene Series (A^s, a^y, a^t)

This gene determines whether a dog will be dark or blonde or a bit of each.

A^s is DOMINANT to all other alleles in the series. It permits *dark* to be distributed over the entire body.

a^y is RECESSIVE to A^s and allows a *blonde* coat to be distributed over the entire body. This allele, however, is dominant to the next allele, a^t.

a^t is the rascal that produces a bi-color such as a black and tan. It is RECESSIVE to both a^y and A^s.

To Produce Black

A^s will give a dog a dark coat, but it will not necessarily be black. It is only if A^s is combined with E that the coat will be black. Change one of the genes and the result will be different—a^ye will be blond with black hairs or it can be a sooty red, known as a sable.

A^s can be dark red without black hairs or a clear red

a^y is blonde without black, so it will be a pale pastel or wheaten

a^tE will be black and tan

a^te will be red and tan

Although seemingly more complicated, the alleles interact in typical Mendelian fashion.

A^sA^see (clear red) mated to a a^ya^yEE (sable) all the first generation puppies will be BLACK, but not homozygotic. Hidden recessive genes will prevent the color from being jet-black due to incomplete dominance. However, if we breed first-generation brother and sister together we should expect out of 16 possibilities, 9 BLACK, 3 RED, 3 SABLE, and 1 WHEATEN. Only one of each color will be homozygous for the color. A^sA^sEE is homozygous dominant black, and a^ya^yee is homozygous recessive wheaten.

The B-Gene Pair (Bb)

Straight Mendelian Bb in action, the gene effects only the dark color.

B equals BLACK

b allows reduced pigment formation in the liver-colored dog.

There are no other alleles of this gene and no other effect. It cannot produce a blue dog with black nose and pigment.

The C-Gene Series (C, c^{ch}, c^e, c^a)

This gene series controls the strength of color of both the DARK and the BLOND.

C is dominant to all other alleles of this gene and gives FULL COLOR STRENGTH. It produces the jet black and white Shih Tzu, so flashy in the ring, providing the dog has B and not b in its genes. It also produces the rich sable or dark tan in blond-coated Shih Tzu.

If a Shih Tzu does not exhibit full strength of color, it cannot carry the dominant C in its genotype and cannot possibly produce it.

The allele c^{ch} is recessive to C but dominant to the other alleles. It will produce the rich color of C but has a distinctly greater effect in

BIS Ch. Bel Air Ace of Spades was bred by Cathie Phillips. He is top-winning all-black Shih Tzu in the breed history. Pictured winning BIS under Maxwell Riddle at Lewis-Clark Kennel Club in May, 1978, he was owner-handled all the way by Diane Backovich.

```
                                          ┌─Jungfaltets Wu-Po
                            ┌─Si Kiang's Gumpy
                            │             └─Si Kiang's Mi Tzi
              Ch. Chateau's Golden Dandy
                            │             ┌─Pa Sha's Charlie Wong
                            └─Su-Linn of La Chateau
                                          └─Sue-Ling Jerome
        Gardner's Black Devil
                            │             ┌─Jungfaltets Wu-Po
                            └─Si Kiang's Gumpy
                                          └─Si Kiang's Mi Tzi
              Gardner's Miss Fanci Pants
                                          ┌─Ch. Si Kiang's Mi Tzu
                            Pa Sha Little Black Sambo
                                          └─Tien of Shu Lin
CH. BEL AIR ACE OF SPADES
                                          ┌─Ch. Sopon Von Tschomo-Lungma
                            Giri Shu v.d. Oranje Manege
                                          └─Ch. Lou Shu v.d. Oranje Manege
              AA-Li-Wang De Kleine Oosterling, R.O.M. (Dutch import)
                                          ┌─Im Pi Shu v.d. Oranje Manege
                            Elfenbloem v.d. Blauwe Mammouth
                                          └─Ra-Ree Wielingor
        Ch. Monki Doodle of Midhill, R.O.M.
                                          ┌─Giri Shu v.d. Oranje Manege
                            AA-Li-Wang de Kleine Oosterling, R.O.M.
                                          └─Elfenbloem v.d. Blauwe Mammouth
              Silverheel Lilli Tu
                                          ┌─Ch. Che Ma Che of Antarctica
                            Antarctica Kung Chu of Darite
                                          └─Fu Chi of Darite
```

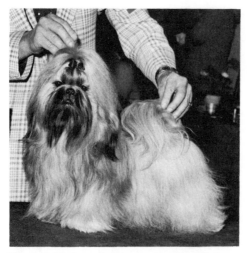

This gold, black-masked dog is a grandson of the
author's all-black Si-Kiang Barban Chee Chee.
He is Ch. Stylistic's Artists Touch, bred by Jo Ann
Webster and Dee Shepherd and owned by Evelyn
Clay.   *Ashbey*

Am./Can. Ch. Pen Sans Cinnamon Toast, owned
by Gloria Busselman, carries desirable, uniform
markings and even distribution of white.

230

A granddaughter of Chee Chee is Ch. Stylistic Good as Gold, owned by Barbara and George Williamson. *Gilbert*

<pre>
                              Char Nick's Mr. Chan
                    Ch. Char Nick's I Gotcha
                              Pakos Lotus Blossom
          Ch. Nanjo Oh Mai Gosh of Char Nick
                              Ch. Char Nick's Sam Chu
                    Ch. Char Nick's Sesame of Sam Chu
                              Car Nick's Kwan Yen Tzu
     Ch. Afshi's Gunther
                              Ch. Mar-Del's Ring-A-Ding-Ding
                    Ch. Paisley Ping Pong
                              Ch. Paisley Petronella
          Afshi's Tekhla
                              Ch. Mar-Del's Chow Mein
                    Ch. Emperor's Adoring Amah
                              Aagalyn's Water Chestnut
CH. STYLISTIC GOOD AS GOLD
                              Int. Ch. Bjorneholm's Pif
                    Am., Can. Ch. Chumulari Ying Ying
                              Int. Ch. Tangra Von Tschomo-Lungma
          Am., Can. Ch. Chumulari Sheng-Li Che
                              Si Kiang's Tashi
                    Chumulari Trari
                              Wei Honey Gold of Elfann
     Ch. Stylistic Barban Scarlet
                              Elfann Fu-Ling of Lhakang
                    Ching-Yea of Lhakang
                              Ching-Yo of Elfann
          Si-Kiang's Barban Chee Chee
                              Si Kiang's Jenn-Wu
                    Si Kiang's Snopy-Snop
                              Si Kiang's Changa
</pre>

reducing the blond color than in effecting black. We see the result of this allele in Shih Tzu with black tippings and/or black masks, while the rest of the coat is reduced in color strength to a gold or pale gold.

The allele c^e produces an extreme dilution and is responsible for the pale or pastel pigmentation, effecting both dark and blond coats. It may produce a red cast to the eye.

The allele c^a produces complete albinism.

What is Albinism?

According to C.C. Little, albinism is caused by an allele of the C-Gene series, the c^a allele which controls the depth of pigmentation. It is recessive to all other forms of this gene. If a dog receives a double recessive, $c^a c^a$, it will have no pigment in either hair, skin or eye. The hair will be pure white, the skin pink, the eyes pink or red. If a Shih Tzu is born white but has blue or dark eyes, it is not a true albino.

Albinism in Shih Tzu is extremely rare, so its existence and cause are theoretical and will remain so until someone can prove Little wrong.

However, we do know that we can have a white coat which is not truly white. It is the extreme dilution of a very light-colored coat, caused by the c^e allele, to make the coat so nearly white that it appears white to the average eye, but is, in reality, pale cream. The effect of a recessive c^e allele on a dark coat has no visible influence.

It is known that white areas will form on Shih Tzu where the genes have ordered the color to withdraw. In cases of extreme dilution, however, the color has not withdrawn—it is there, but in such a dilute form that it is not visible to the eye. Albinism, on the other hand has no color in the first place to be ordered by the genes to withdraw.

The D-Gene Pair (Dd)

This gene is the dilution or density gene seen only in dark coats and is pure Mendelian in action. The dominant D produces intense pigment.

The recessive d produces the blue as seen in Chow Chows, Poodles, Greyhounds and Weimaraners. If the B gene is also present, the pigment will be black, but if the gene b is present, as it is in Weimaraners, the pigment will be liver.

Since other genes also produce blue coats, one can tell when it is caused by the dd gene in animals because of the quality of coat, often described as silvery. It has a peculiar flat or dull quality.

The E-Gene Series (E^m, E e^{br}, e)

The E dominant in this series permits black hairs to be present all over the coat both in dark areas and in blond areas. The series also

232

Ch. Lou Wan Shanghai Lilly, proudly owned and handled by Wanda Gec, was BB at the Providence County KC under the author, Ann Seranne. *Gilbert*

Ch. Truro's Command Performance, bred by Cheryl Crane and William Paelko, Jr., is owned by Mr. and Mrs. John Wilus IV and shown by John. Sired by Ch. Mandarin's Oliver Twist he is out of Ch. Gunning's Frito Bandito. *Ashbey*

includes a black mask allele, which may be a sort of superextension factor, which makes E^m dominant to all other members of the E series including E, which is dominant to the other alleles in this series.

E^m causes the black mask typically seen in Pugs, Afghans, Pekingese and Shih Tzu.

e^{br} causes a brindle effect. The gene is recessive to E^m and E, but dominant to e.

e is recessive to $E^m E$ and e^{br} and permits no black hairs in a coat.

At this point I think a few examples might be in order to bring us up to date before proceeding with the remaining color genes.

1. A dog with A^s (dark coat) will be BLACK only if it has also the E gene. If it has the e recessive the coat will not be black but a rich dark Irish Setter red. The results are the same with a bi-colored dog or a genetic a^t.

2. A dog with a blond coat (a^y) will be RED if it also carries the E, but will be more of a sooty red or sable than the pure red coat of a dog which is genetically $A^s e$, and again, the same is true of the bi-colored Shih Tzu or the $a^t E$ or the $a^t e$.

The recessive e will cause a blond coat to lighten to a tan or yellow. Other genes will also influence the depth of color but, setting those aside for the moment, we can conclude that: $A^s E$ = BLACK; $A^s e$ = CLEAR RED; $a^y E$ = SOOTY RED; $a^y e$ = ORANGISH TANNISH YELLOW.

We also know that if we mate two red parents, one genotypically $A^s e$ and the other $a^y E$, we can come up with $A^s E$ or BLACK PUPPIES or $A^y e$ or ORANGE, YELLOW, TAN PUPPIES.

Other colors can also appear, of course, depending on what other recessive or hypostatic forms of the A and E genes are present in the genotype of the dogs mated.

The *G*-Gene Pair *(Gg)*

Once more we have a pair of simple Mendelian genes. The dominant G causes greying of the coat with age. If a dog inherits the recessive d, there will be no greying that occurs with age.

It is thought that this gene is responsible for the blue coat color of the mature Kerry Blue and Bedlington Terrier.

This gene has no effect on the color of the pigmentation of eye or nose.

The *M*-Gene Pair *(Mm)*

This is a gene to watch closely in some breeds. The M dominant causes the Merle or Dapple effect in Collies or harlequin Great Danes. Fortunately most other dog breeds do not have the gene at all, or if

Ch. Hodari Imperial Lin, 11-month-old bitch, was Best in Sweepstakes at the Southern California Shih Tzu Specialty, but her show career did not stop there. She was WB at Westminster in 1977 and quickly completed her championship. She was shown in Best of Breed competition eight times in five weeks, winning seven BB and six Group placements to become No. 9 Shih Tzu for the year. Bred and owned by Laurie Battey, her sire was Ch. Winward's Wheeler Dealer, and her dam was Ch. Hodari Tam Lin.   *Yuhl*

Ch. Hodari Lord of the Rings (Ch. Lainee Sigmond Floyd ex Ch. Hodari Imperial Lin), bred and owned by Laurie Battey was RD at the 1979 Southern California Specialty, scoring from the 6–9 puppy class. Enroute to the title, he also had a 5-point major from the puppy class.   *Yuhl*

they do, they have the double recessive *mm*, which has no merling or dappling effect.

Should a dog receive a double dose of the dominant *MM* it will usually be all white, deaf and/or blind and generally sterile. So it is usually a self-eliminating gene if the double dominant *MM* is received.

The *P*-Gene Pair

Another pure action Mendelian pair is rare in most breeds of dogs, but it is present in Pekingese and could, therefore be present in some Shih Tzu.

The dominant *P* has no effect whatsoever on coat color.

The recessive *p*, however is analogous to a similar gene in mice or guinea pigs where it leaves a blond coat unchanged but radically reduces the pigment in dark coats. Black coats or black areas become silver or lilac colored, and liver areas become a silver fawn or champagne.

The rare combination of a double recessive *pp*, causes the eye color of a dog to become pink or ruby. It is known as the Pink Eye Dilution double recessive.

The *S*-Gene Series (*S*, *s^i*, *s^p*, *s^w*)

This is a fascinating color gene series, but due to modifiers plus and modifiers minus, incomplete dominance and other mind-boggling variations, an elusive one to determine from the phenotype of a dog.

The *S* is dominant to the other alleles. It will produce a solid-colored coat without any white areas at all. And this is where a modifier comes in. It just might allow a touch of white or a spot, or enough to confuse the *S* with the first allele the *S^i*.

In breeds where such a spot is a fault, as in Poodles, the breeder should bear in mind that if a spot appears, the dog will not be able to pass on a solid-colored coat to its progeny UNLESS mated to a dog that is dominant in that color.

The allele *s^i* stands for Irish Spotting and is recessive only to *S*. Consistent areas of white are characteristic of this allele as personified in the Basenji. Such definite areas of white can produce a strikingly flashy black and white Shih Tzu. But again, modifiers can increase white areas, sometimes forming an extended pattern which fuses to produce a white collar linking chest and forelegs and known as the "Collie Pattern."

The most common areas on the dog where the color withdraws and pure white appears are on the muzzle, forehead as a star or blaze, chest, belly, tail tip and on one or more feet.

236

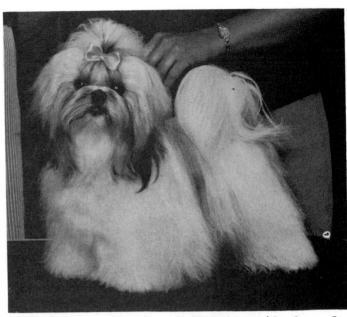

Ch. Sing Hi's Sweet Chariot (Ch. Hai Sing A-Hi Song of Pen Sans ex Pen Sans Aphrodite), owned by Charles and Vera Hayward and bred by Mrs. Hayward and Jane Jones. "Cheerie" finished in 12 shows over two months and a month before her sire became a champion. *Lindemaier*

Ch. Bel Air Irresistible O' Bambo is well named for many judges found her exactly that. She completed her championship at 12 months with two Group two placements. She was owned by Diane Backovich, and shown by both Diane and her breeder Cathie Phillips. *Lindemaier*

237

Ch. Lisel's Rock 'N Rye finished from the bred-by-exhibitor class, with four majors and a Best of Breed over champions. He won his first points from the puppy class at seven months. "Rocky's" pedigree illustrates the doubling on the genes of a great ancestor and doubling again and again. Actually there are eight crosses in the 5-generation pedigree back to Ch. Chumulari Ying Ying. Count 'em!

Ch. Mar-Del's Ring-A-Ding-Ding

Ch. Paisley Ping Pong

Ch. Paisley Petronella

Ch. Cabrand's Midnight Special

Ch. Mariljac Maripet

Cabrand's Cara of Lou Wan

Fortune Cookie of Lou Wan

Ch. Lou Wan Midnight Son

Ch. Mei Tu of Lou Wan

Ch. Lou Wan Casinova

Fortune Cookie of Lou Wan

Ch. Lou Wan Mariposa of Sarifan

Ch. Chumulari Sheng Li Che

Chumulari Tai Tai Mei Ling

Can. Ch. Carrimount Tai Tai Chumulari

CH. LISEL'S ROCK 'N RYE

Ch. Chumulari Ying Ying

Am., Can. Ch. Chumulari Sheng Li Che

Chumulari Trari

Chumulari Chin Chi

Ch. Chumulari Ying Ying

Can. Ch. Carrimount Tai Tai Chumulari

Ch. Brownhills' Yolan of Greenmoss

Ch. Lisel's Eleanor Rigby

Int. Ch. Bjorneholm's Pif

Int. Ch. Ollo Von Tschomo-Lungma

Int. Ch. Bjorneholm's Ting-A-Ling

Ima Shu v.d. Oranje Manege

Huang Ti of Lhakang

Fengli Shu v.d. Oranje Manege

Am. Int., Dutch, world Ch. Zim Shu v.d. Oranje Manege

Ch. Mar-Del's Chow Mein
Mar-Del's Snow Pea
Ch. Mar-Del's Chow Mein
Pitti-Sing of Sangchen
Ch. Chumulari Ying Ying
Mariljac Cha Boom
Ch. Chumulari Ying Ying
Ch. Chumulari Mei Mei
Ch. Chumulari Ying Ying
Ch. Chumulari Ping Chu
Ch. Chumulari Ying Ying
Ch. Chumulari Mei Mei
Ch. Chumulari Ying Ying
Chumulari Trari
Ch. Chumulari Ying Ying
Ch. Brownhills' Yolan of
Greenmoss
Int. Ch. Bjorneholm's Pif
Int. Ch. Tangra V. Tschomo-
Lungma
Si Kiang's Tashi
Wei Honey Gold of Elfann
Int. Ch. Bjorneholm's Pif
Int. Ch. Tangra V. Tschomo-
Lungma
Choo T'Sun of Telota
Brownhills' Cindy
Int. Ch. Bjorneholm's Wu-Ling
Ranga Ling
Int. Ch. Bjorneholm's Wu-Ling
Ch. Bjorneholm's Bolette
Juan of Lhakang
Hwa Yin of Lhakang
Int. Ch. Ollo V. Tschomo-Lungma
Geltree Mao Hsueh

The True White

The white found in the Irish Spotting s^i allele should not be confused with any tendency toward albinism (c^a) where all pigment is lacking, nor with the white dilution allele c^e where color is still there, but in such a diluted form that it is visible as cream or not visible at all to the eye.

At least two genes are responsible for commanding the withdrawal of color from specific areas, resulting in a true white. One of these genes is the multiple allele S-gene with its modifiers which can cause minor deviations from the norm. The other is the straight Mendelian Tt gene which we will come to.

The S-Gene Series, continued

s^p, the next allele in order of strength is the s^p of the piebald spotting gene, recessive to both S and s^i. It causes the color to withdraw from colored areas anywhere in a range of 15 to 85 percent of the entire coat. The span range is due again to modifiers. Irish Spotting is typified by the Beagle and is prevalent in Cockers, Springers and Pointers.

As long as Shih Tzu breeders and judges prefer uniform markings, this gene, easily recognized by the irregularity of markings, should be eliminated by simply placing such pups in pet homes.

The s^w allele is recessive to all others and is responsible for extreme white piebalds as found in the Bull Terrier and the Sealyham, where only a patch of pigmented coat appears occasionally in an otherwise white breed. The patches are usually near the eye, ear or on the tail. The pigment on such dogs carrying the s^w remains dark and on an all-white Shih Tzu with black nose and dark brown eyes might be stunning in the show ring.

The T-Gene Pair

This is the "ticking" gene and is simple Mendelian in action.

T is responsible for pigmented spots on a white background as found in Dalmatians, Pointers, English Setters and in some hounds. The spots generally do not appear before the pups are at least three to four weeks old and often much later in the long-coated breeds.

Hopefully Shih Tzu breeders will prevent this T dominant gene from creeping into their genotypes and will remain with the tt so that no spotting or ticking will mar the beauty of the color pattern of our present-day Shih Tzu. Fortunately it is a dominant one and as such could easily be eliminated from a line should it appear, as genes are apt to do, in often unexpected fashion.

240

This perky little stud dog is Am. and Can. Ch. Sanchis Vhima, sire of BIS X-Rated owned by Elaine Meltzer. He is shown with handler Ray Wine. *Graham*

Am/Can. Ch. Dun-Kee-Wang Socket Tu-Ya, R.O.M. (Ch. Dun-Kee-Wang de Kleine Osterling ex Cooper's Sokatina) bred, owned and shown by Al Marcum. She earned her Canadian championship at 11 months and her American championship at 14 months. She is on the all-time, top-producing list of bitches, tying for third place with seven champions. She was top-producing bitch in 1975 and again in 1977. *Petrulis*

Little did anyone realize, at the time this picture was taken, that this winsome puppy would grow and develop into the first Shih Tzu in the United States to win a Best in Show. Can you guess who it is? Right! It's Am/Can. Ch. Chumulari Ying Ying, R.O.M. at three months of age.

A bewitching head study of the all-black Ch. Timerlakes Rocky Vollee Ki Ki, bred by Helen Mueller and proudly owned and shown all the way to his championship by Molly Heck. He completed his championship requirements on November 8, 1979, a day that Molly will never forget! *Heck*

One of Ying Ying's many champions is Can. Ch. Chumulari Li Jen out of Chumulari Dorje. This lovely Shih Tzu, owned by E. Joyce Harris in Canada, illustrates the striking black-tipping on the ears.

Ch. Din Ho Wind Jammer of Ric Mar, with his chrysanthemum head, straight topline and gay tail, shows his potential show qualities as early as four months of age. He won his first points from puppy class the first time shown. He finished with major wins at Tuxedo Park and Westchester at 14 months of age, shown by Emily Gunning.   *Hoyt*

243

So What Color Genes Should be in our Shih Tzu?

The pastel-colored Shih Tzu can be quite softly beautiful but will never be as strikingly dramatic as the darker, more vibrantly-colored animals.

The light shades are caused by c^{ch} and c^e. However both these alleles are recessive to the undiluted pigmentation of C, which produces the dark, rich colors. This dominant C cannot be "hidden" or masked by the other c series alleles. So for intensely pigmented Shih Tzu, keep the C coming along from one generation to the next.

The dominant S will give a solid-colored coat, which in itself can be very lovely, such as a rich gold (A^se) and especially if these alleles are combined with E^m and therefore has the black mask and black tippings.

Perhaps the second most attractive coat coloration is caused by the s^i or Irish Spotting allele, and is most effective in the black and white Shih Tzu. Here, however, the breeder must be constantly alert for modifiers or the introduction of s^p or piebalding allele which can upset the balance of pigmented to unpigmented coat, increasing the white areas and producing white in undesirable areas.

Major Barre Hasle's Shih Tzu

At this point I would like to give credit to Major Barre Hasle's most illuminating articles on the inheritance of color in a series of four articles published in the *Shih Tzu News* in 1975. Without them, I doubt if I would ever have been able to understand the basis of coat color inheritance.

It should also be pointed out that Major Hasle's theories are by no means certainties. Like the conjectures and theories of other scientists, they are only probabilities, for the simple reason that there is nothing certain in the science of genetics. Major Hasle has however, when combined with Gregor Mendel's Laws, given us the genetic tools for maintaining self-color, the "Collie" pattern and pure white (not albino).

I take the liberty of quoting from one of his articles—

> I think the genetic make-up of MY Shih Tzu would be Ss^is^w. To reach this, as a breeder, I would NEVER USE a dog or bitch with irregular distribution of white—the hall-mark of s^p. However, s^p can be carried hidden as it is recessive to S and s^i and I would suspect its presence when the white areas are extensive EVEN if the pattern is regular. When s^p is bred out I would have SS, homozygous SELF-COLORED showing no or very little white; Ss^i, heterozygous SELF-COLORED which could be without white, but incomplete dominance plus modifiers could give it white in the typical s^i places but probably not a full collar. (It would not breed true); s^is^i, homozygous IRISH SPOTTING including the Collie

Michael Lannie with Ch. Khantinka's The Great Pumpkin, owned by Joe and Pinky Edwards. "Pumpkin" was sired by Ch. Dragonwyck The Great Gatsby out of Reina vom Tschomo-Lungma.

Jean Lade guided Ch. Nanjo Wild Honey to Best of Breed at Old Dominion KC under Katherine Gately. "Honey," owned by breeder Joan Cowie, is by Ch. Char-Nick's Swing Erh of Copa out of Nanjo Wildfire. *Wm. Gilbert*

245

Pattern. By selective breeding through generations, the areas of white might increase beyond what could be called the typical pattern; and $s^w s^w$, homozygous WHITE.*

SUMMATION—The Language of Color Genetics

				E^m					
A	B	C	D	E	G	M	P	S	T
A^s	b	c^{ch}	d	e^{br}	g	m	p	s^i	t
a^y		c^e		e				s^p	
a^t		c^a						s^w	

Summation Reference Chart

A stands for AREAS OF DARK OR BLOND

A^s = all dark coat

a^y = all blond coat

a^t = bi-color (tan points)

Bb stands for BLACK OR BROWN

B = black

b = liver

C stands for COLOR STRENGTH AND FULL DEPTH OF PIG-MENT

c^{ch} = chinchilla color or a reduced pigmentation

c^e = extreme reduction of pigment

c^a = albinism

Dd stands for DILUTION TO MALTESE BLUE*

D = normal color

d = blue* (the long, silky, blue-grey of the Maltese cat)

E stands for EXTENSION OF BLACK HAIR. It permits black pigmented hairs in a blond coat.

E^m = black mask and/or tippings

e^{br} = brindle

e = no black at all, even in a dark coat

Gg stands for GREYING or fading with age. This is NOT a true blue

G = greying with age

g = no greying with age, the coat maintains its color

Mm stands for MERLE (usually blue-grey with flecks of black)

M = merling

m = no merling

*Major Hasle wrote earlier that he had never seen a real WHITE SHIH TZU with full pigmented nose and eyes. He has heard about them and feels they must be just breath-taking. I agree.

Ch. Hai Tai Honey of Kathmandu, handled by William Cunningham, is shown winning BB at Licking River (Ohio). Norman Patton, the judge, was a professional for years, and one of the best. "Honey" was sired by Ch. Emperors Life of the Party out of Kathmandu's Plum Blossom. She is owned by Racille Karelitz and was bred by **Racille and Susan Mechem.** *Alverson*

Ch. Chateau's Sans Souci of Jolei, an all-black Shih Tzu, became a champion at 11½ months with eight of his necessary 15 points won from the puppy class. Owner-handler Diane Kijowski campaigned him to his title as skillfully as any professional. At 2½ years, Diane guided "Blaka" all the way to a BIS. They are pictured here winning one of their five Toy Group firsts. "Blaka" was bred by Billie Forsman, sired by Ch. Emperor's Ebony Bla-Ka-Moor, out of Chateau's Tus and Tuk.

Top-Winning Bitch in 1979 and winner of the coveted Elfann Trophy is BIS Ch. Kung Fu's We're Happy with Gunning, bred by David Tucker and owned by Wendell Brewer, David Lehman and Emily Gunning. Her total wins include one Best in Show, one Specialty Best in Show and numerous Groups. She is pictured winning the Toy Group at the Sara-Bay KC under Edna Ackerman, handled by Wendell Brewer.

Graham

```
                              Jungfaltets Wu-Po
                      Ch. Mar-Del's Chow Mein
                              Si Kiang's Mi Tzi
                  Ch. Mar-Del's Ring-A-Ding-Ding
                              Jungfaltets Wu-Po
                      Mar-Del's Snow Pea
                              Si Kiang's Madam Wu
          Ch. Charjalong's Bronze Bandit (go/wh)
                              Ch. Chumulari Ying Ying
                      Ch. Carrimount Ah Chop Chop
                              Ch. Brownhills' Yolan of Greenmoss
                  Ch. Long's Heide Ho Ah Chop Chop
                              Yam-Yam of Marlen
                      Ch. Long's Little Lick
                              Shaadar's the Mosaci Empress
CH. KUNG FU'S HAPPI WITH GUNNING (go/wh)
                              Ch. Mar-Del's Chow Mein
                      Ch. Mar-Del's Ring-A-Ding-Ding
                              Mar-Del's Snow Pea
                  Ch. Paisley Ping Pong
                              Ch. Mar-Del's Chow Mein
                      Ch. Paisley Petronella
                              Pitti-Sing of Sangchen
          Ch. Nanjo Ping's Pa-Ti-Cake (blk/wh)
                              Ch. Si Shu v.d. Oranje Manege
                      Ch. Parquin's Sarrtezza
                              Lakoya's Lu Lu
                  Sinarra of Parquin's
                              Parquin's Gogay
                      Parquin's Sintarra
                              Parquin's M. Emer
```

Ch. Mysty Dai Masumi, bred and owned by Dorothy Poole. "Masumi" received all her championship points from the bred by exhibitor class and earned her title just before her first birthday. During this short show career she won four Bests of Breed, two of these over champions.

```
                                    Aagalyn's Charlie of Glen
                        Ch. Glen's Fina Lee
                                    Aagalyn's Honey Bunch
                   Mandarin's Madrigal
                                    Ch. Char Nìck's I Gotcha
                        ┌Ch. Mandarin's Royale Rhapsody
                        │           Ch. Mandarin's Buttercup
        Ch. Pinafore Minstrel of Mandarin
                        │           Ch. Greenmoss Gilliigan
                        │ Can. Ch. Winemaker's Candiman
                        │           Ch. Northshire's Bit O'Honey
                        Ch. Mandarin's Sassy Samantha
                        │           Ch. Char Nick's I Gotcha
                        └Ch. Mandarin's Royale Rhapsody
                                    Ch. Mandarin's Buttercup
CH. MYSTY DAI MASUMI (go/wh)
                                    Ch. Golden Peregrine of Elfann
                        Ch. Greenmoss Golden Frolic of Elfann
                                    Elfann Sunshine of Greenmoss
                   Ch. Carrimount Ah Tiko Tiko
                                    Chao T'Sun of Telota
                        Ch. Brownhills' Yolan of Greenmoss
                                    Brownhills' Cindy
        Ambelon Mysty Dai
                                    Carrimount Ah Chop Chop
                        Ch. Long's Chiny Chin Ah Chop Chop
                        ┌Ch. Long's Little Lick
                   Ch. Sparkle Plenty for David
                        │  Ch. Bernett's Ming Toi
                        Long's Kiko Lady
                        └Ch. Long's Little Lick
```

Pp stands for PINK EYE DILUTION

    P = no effect on coat color

    p = radical reduction of dark pigment; leaves blond coats unaltered; eye color is pink or ruby.

S stands for SOLID OR SELF-COLORED (an absence of white)

    s^i = Irish spotting or the regular distribution of color and white.

    s^p = piebald spotting or irregular distribution of color and white.

    s^w = extreme white spotting or almost all white

Tt stands for TICKING or small spots of color in white areas

    T = ticking

    t = no ticking

Specific Color Breeding

Many Shih Tzu breeders have, I am sure, done a great deal of experimental color breeding but their results or conclusions have never been published.

The first attempt at color breeding, according to Audrey Dadds, was carried out by Audrey Fowler of Chasmu. One of the earliest Shih Tzu breeders, whose kennel was established in 1938, Mrs. Fowler set out to establish a gold line. However, she had no progeny from her early gold and white imports from China with which to achieve this.

Her foundation dog was a gold/white grandson of the Swedish Choo Choo, Sui Yan. Although he was registered as a black and white, he did have some brown on him. Sui Yan was bred to Madam Ko of Taishan, a chocolate/white bitch and a granddaughter of the brown/white imported Tashi of Chouette. The ensuing litter included two bitches: liver/white Ta Chi of Taishan (the first champion of the breed in England) and gold/white Yi, who became the foundation of the Chasmu strain.

Yi was mated to Ch. Choo Ling and the only offspring was a black and white bitch, named Om Mani Pudni. When bred back to her white/gold grandsire, Sui Yan, she produced many solid honey and honey/white colored Shih Tzu with excellent pigmentation. Among these was the dog Ki Ming.

Om Mani Pudni was then mated to the black Shebo Shunde Of Hungjao, of the solid-colored Ishuh line; there were some honey-colored specimens, but in those, where the gold had darkened, it also blended with black. As a result most of the puppies were a solid dark gold/brindle. One, Kepong, was solid black.

In 1954 one of this litter, a white/honey bitch, Golden Salween,

When Madrigal was bred to his full sister, "Samantha," he produced Am/Can/Berm. Ch. Pinafore Minstrel of Madrigal, a bitch, and Ch. Pinafore's Minstrel of Mandarin, a dog owned by Dorothy Poole. Born in 1977 they trace their illustrious ancestry back to some of the early "greats."

Ashbey

```
                              Ch. Mar-Del's Moo Goo Gai Pan (blk/wh)
                    Aagalyn's Charlie of Glen
                    Aagalyn's Patchee
          Ch. Glen's Fina Lee (red brin/wh)
                              Ch. Aagalyn's Ying Yang (go/wh)
                    Aagalyn's Honey Bunch
                    Aagalyn's Ann
     Mandarin's Madrigal (go/wh)
                              Char Nick's Mr. Chan (red/wh)
                    ┌─Ch. Char Nick's I Gotcha (go/wh)
                    │         Pakos Lotus Blossom (blk/wh)
          ┌─Ch. Mandarin's Royale Rhapsody (red brin/wh)
          │         │         Ch. Royale Hu Lu (sil/wh)
          │         └─Ch. Mandarin's Buttercup (past sil/go/wh)
          │                   Cottonmop's Daisy Mae (red brin/wh)
CH. PINAFORE MINSTREL OF MANDARIN
```

(An interesting example of a half-brother ex half-sister mating through the granddam, Ch. Mandarin's Royale Rhapsody.)

```
                              Ch. Golden Peregrine of Elfann
                    Ch. Greenmoss Gilligan
                    Jasmine of Greenmoss
          Can Ch. Winemaker's Candiman
                              Ch. Ho Tai of Greenmoss
                    Ch. Northshire's Bit O'Honey
                    Ch. Greenmoss Jezebel
     Ch. Mandarin's Sassy Samantha
                              Char Nick's Mr. Chan
                    └─Ch. Char Nick's I Gotcha
                              Pakos Lotus Blossom
          └─Ch. Mandarin's Royale Rhapsody
                              Ch. Royale Hu Lu
                    └─Ch. Mandarin's Buttercup
                              Cottonmop's Daisy Mae
```

was mated to her half brother, Ki Ming, and produced the desired clear gold in a dog named Tasmin, who established this color when bred to an equally clear gold bitch, Lhakang Mimosa of Northallerton. The kennel is still noted for this color today. The experimental breedings suggest that gold is genetically recessive and when a dog and bitch of clear gold are mated together, all their offspring will be clear gold.

Sui Yan (go/wh)

Ki Ming (honey/wh)
       Ch. Choo Ling
Om Mani Pudni (brin/wh)
       Yi (go/wh)
Golden Tasmin (clr gold)

    *Sui Yan
    **Madam Ko of Taishan (choc/wh)

Shebo Schunde of Hungjao (blk)

Golden Salween (honey/wh)

Om Mani Pudni

Leo Lao of Lhakang (go/wh)

Shebo Tsemo of Lhakang (red/brn/grey)

Me of Lhakang (go/wh)

Lhakang Mimosa of Northallerton (clr gold)

†Wu Cheng of Lhakang (blk/wh)

Lotze of Lhakang (go/wh)

†Mao Wong of Lhakang

CHASMU color experiments indicating clear gold is a recessive and will breed true. All puppies resulting from this breeding were CLEAR GOLD.

*Grandson of Swedish-bred Choo Choo
**Granddaughter of Tashi of Chouette (brn/wh)
†Full brother ex full sister mating

BIBLIOGRAPHY

LL OWNERS of pure-bred dogs will benefit themselves and their dogs by enriching their knowledge of breeds
nd of canine care, training, breeding, psychology and other important aspects of dog management. The follow-
g list of books covers further reading recommended by judges, veterinarians, breeders, trainers and other authorities.
ooks may be obtained at the finer book stores and pet shops, or through Howell Book House Inc., publishers,
ew York.

BREED BOOKS

FGHAN HOUND, Complete	Miller & Gilbert
IREDALE, New Complete	Edwards
KITA, Complete	Linderman & Funk
LASKAN MALAMUTE, Complete	Riddle & Seeley
ASSET HOUND, New Complete	Braun
LOODHOUND, Complete	Brey & Reed
OXER, Complete	Denlinger
RITTANY SPANIEL, Complete	Riddle
ULLDOG, New Complete	Hanes
ULL TERRIER, New Complete	Eberhard
AIRN TERRIER, New Complete	Marvin
HESAPEAKE BAY RETRIEVER, Complete	Cherry
HIHUAHUA, Complete	Noted Authorities
OCKER SPANIEL, New	Kraeuchi
OLLIE, New	Official Publication of the Collie Club of America
ACHSHUND, The New	Meistrell
ALMATIAN, The	Treen
OBERMAN PINSCHER, New	Walker
NGLISH SETTER, New Complete	Tuck, Howell & Graef
NGLISH SPRINGER SPANIEL, New	Goodall & Gasow
OX TERRIER, New	Nedell
ERMAN SHEPHERD DOG, New Complete	Bennett
ERMAN SHORTHAIRED POINTER, New	Maxwell
OLDEN RETRIEVER, New Complete	Fischer
ORDON SETTER, Complete	Look
REAT DANE, New Complete	Noted Authorities
REAT DANE, The—Dogdom's Apollo	Draper
REAT PYRENEES, Complete	Strang & Giffin
RISH SETTER, New Complete	Eldredge & Vanacore
RISH WOLFHOUND, Complete	Starbuck
ACK RUSSELL TERRIER, Complete	Plummer
EESHOND, New Complete	Cash
ABRADOR RETRIEVER, New Complete	Warwick
HASA APSO, Complete	Herbel
MALTESE, Complete	Cutillo
MASTIFF, History and Management of the	Baxter & Hoffman
MINIATURE SCHNAUZER, New	Kiedrowski
EWFOUNDLAND, New Complete	Chern
ORWEGIAN ELKHOUND, New Complete	Wallo
LD ENGLISH SHEEPDOG, Complete	Mandeville
EKINGESE, Quigley Book of	Quigley
EMBROKE WELSH CORGI, Complete	Sargent & Harper
OODLE, New	Irick
OODLE CLIPPING AND GROOMING BOOK, Complete	Kalstone
ORTUGUESE WATER DOG, Complete	Braund & Miller
OTTWEILER, Complete	Freeman
AMOYED, New Complete	Ward
COTTISH TERRIER, New Complete	Marvin
HETLAND SHEEPDOG, The New	Riddle
HIH TZU, Joy of Owning	Seranne
HIH TZU, The (English)	Dadds
IBERIAN HUSKY, Complete	Demidoff
ERRIERS, The Book of All	Marvin
VEIMARANER, Guide to the	Burgoin
VEST HIGHLAND WHITE TERRIER, Complete	Marvin
VHIPPET, Complete	Pegram
ORKSHIRE TERRIER, Complete	Gordon & Bennett

BREEDING

RT OF BREEDING BETTER DOGS, New	Onstott
REEDING YOUR OWN SHOW DOG	Seranne
OW TO BREED DOGS	Whitney
OW PUPPIES ARE BORN	Prine
NHERITANCE OF COAT COLOR IN DOGS	Little

CARE AND TRAINING

BEYOND BASIC DOG TRAINING	Bauman
COUNSELING DOG OWNERS, Evans Guide for	Evans
DOG OBEDIENCE, Complete Book of	Saunders
NOVICE, OPEN AND UTILITY COURSES	Saunders
DOG CARE AND TRAINING FOR BOYS AND GIRLS	Saunders
DOG NUTRITION, Collins Guide to	Collins
DOG TRAINING FOR KIDS	Benjamin
DOG TRAINING, Koehler Method of	Koehler
DOG TRAINING Made Easy	Tucker
GO FIND! Training Your Dog to Track	Davis
GROOMING DOGS FOR PROFIT	Gold
GUARD DOG TRAINING, Koehler Method of	Koehler
MOTHER KNOWS BEST—The Natural Way to Train Your Dog	Benjamin
OPEN OBEDIENCE FOR RING, HOME AND FIELD, Koehler Method of	Koehler
STONE GUIDE TO DOG GROOMING FOR ALL BREEDS	Stone
SUCCESSFUL DOG TRAINING, The Pearsall Guide to	Pearsall
TEACHING DOG OBEDIENCE CLASSES—Manual for Instructors	Volhard & Fisher
TOY DOGS, Kalstone Guide to Grooming All	Kalstone
TRAINING THE RETRIEVER	Kersley
TRAINING TRACKING DOGS, Koehler Method of	Koehler
TRAINING YOUR DOG—Step by Step Manual	Volhard & Fisher
TRAINING YOUR DOG TO WIN OBEDIENCE TITLES	Morsell
TRAIN YOUR OWN GUN DOG, How to	Goodall
UTILITY DOG TRAINING, Koehler Method of	Koehler
VETERINARY HANDBOOK, Dog Owner's Home	Carlson & Giffin

GENERAL

A DOG'S LIFE	Burton & Allaby
AMERICAN KENNEL CLUB 1884-1984—A Source Book	American Kennel Club
CANINE TERMINOLOGY	Spira
COMPLETE DOG BOOK, The	Official Publication of American Kennel Club
DOG IN ACTION, The	Lyon
DOG BEHAVIOR, New Knowledge of	Pfaffenberger
DOG JUDGE'S HANDBOOK	Tietjen
DOG PSYCHOLOGY	Whitney
DOGSTEPS, The New	Elliott
DOG TRICKS	Haggerty & Benjamin
EYES THAT LEAD—Story of Guide Dogs for the Blind	Tucker
FRIEND TO FRIEND—Dogs That Help Mankind	Schwartz
FROM RICHES TO BITCHES	Shattuck
HAPPY DOG/HAPPY OWNER	Siegal
IN STITCHES OVER BITCHES	Shattuck
JUNIOR SHOWMANSHIP HANDBOOK	Brown & Mason
OUR PUPPY'S BABY BOOK (blue or pink)	
SUCCESSFUL DOG SHOWING, Forsyth Guide to	Forsyth
WHY DOES YOUR DOG DO THAT?	Bergman
WILD DOGS in Life and Legend	Riddle
WORLD OF SLED DOGS, From Siberia to Sport Racing	Coppinger